One Hundred Jobs

One Hundred Jobs

A PANORAMA OF WORK IN THE AMERICAN CITY

Ron Howell

PHOTOGRAPHS BY Ozier Muhammad

THE NEW PRESS, NEW YORK

Published in the United States by The New Press, New York
Distributed by W. W. Norton & Company, Inc., New York
Printed in Canada
9 8 7 6 5 4 3 2 1

Library of Congress Cataloging-in-Publication Data

Howell, Ron.
    One hundred jobs: a panorama of work in the American city / Ron Howell;
photographs by Ozier Muhammad.
       p.   cm.
    ISBN 1-56584-430-0 (pbk.)
      1. Vocational guidance—New York (State)—New York.
    2. Occupations—New York (State)—New York case studies. I. Title.
    HF5382.5.U6N37 2000
    331.7'02'09747—dc21 99–23756

The New Press was established in 1990 as a not-for-profit alternative to the large,
commercial publishing houses currently dominating the book publishing industry.
The New Press operates in the public interest rather than for private gain,
and is committed to publishing, in innovative ways, works of educational, cultural,
and community value that are often deemed insufficiently profitable.

www.thenewpress.com

In memory of Joseph Wood, Jr.

CONTENTS

INTRODUCTION

Recently my buddy Ed called to say he had quit his job so he could care for his dying mother. Even in such somber moments, Ed would shun the word "job" and instead use the term "gig," defined in the dictionary as a professional engagement, of short or uncertain duration, such as a jazz performance. In this view of the world, moms endure forever in our minds, but jobs come and go, whimsically often, like extemporized riffs in a musical composition.

It was with whimsy that I set about reporting *One Hundred Jobs*, although when the late editor Joe Wood first approached me about doing the book, I feared it might be too much like a glossary, a compilation of titles and salaries with definitions and pictures. But I quickly saw I could pack a lot into 500 words per job, maybe even a little humor and drama. I realized, too, that I could have fun in choosing people to fill the pages. Yes, I'd get a cross-section of workers and jobs, but I would also pick folks who struck my fancy, like the full-time magician who is the first entry in the book. My ardor for doing *One Hundred Jobs* greatly increased when my good friend Ozier Muhammad, a Pulitzer Prize–winning photographer, agreed to join me. The result of our partnership is this panorama of work in urban America.

I did not research this book, I reported it. I went into offices, neighborhoods, and homes all around the city, and got people to talk to me about what they do to earn a living. Sometimes I found workers in the yellow pages, as I did the exterminator. Other times a phone call would lead to a source who would lead to another source, and on and on for weeks, until someone agreed to be interviewed. Occasionally I just prowled the city looking for people doing interesting things. As for the pictures that accompany the stories, Ozier and I frequently went out together, but most often he would photograph the worker after I had interviewed him or her. (I took pictures in several instances where I knew Ozier would not be able to easily find the person, such as the homeless bottle-collector.) It is important to me that people know all this, because reporting has been my own line of work for more than two decades. To prove it, I have gray hairs and a mushed brain from the years of trying to listen, speed-write, and think of a follow-up question, all at once.

For the most part, I obtained salaries and other data in this book directly from the mouths of the workers I interviewed. But often some nagging doubt made me search databases or check with appropriate sources to ensure that the figures were realistic. Especially problematic were self-employed people who would inflate or deflate their income, for reasons ranging from ego (a concern that associates or relatives might think them a failure for making so little) to fear of the Internal Revenue Service (which might go after them after learning that they made so much). In those cases, I would ask them to give me at least a reasonable income range.

Over the year and a half that Ozier and I worked on *One Hundred Jobs*, I taught journalism at Long Island University and was a contract writer for *Newsday*. I often felt my schedule was grueling, like those of many people in the book. Ozier had to fulfill his duties as a staff photographer with the *New York Times*, and he and his wife Lisa also coped with the lengthy illness of their little daughter Pilar, who thankfully is now recovering.

Doing this book, therefore, has made me think about what it means to have a balanced life. Everyone must work. This platitude has been turned into fact—for everyone but the rich—by politicians who believe only they and a few others should draw from the public till. But at what price do we take anything that "puts bread on the table"? The old jazz term *gigging* implies a unity of body and mind; it suggests a synthesis that allows a person to work and then give time to family and friends, in the universal striving for harmony between a person and his community. This happiness factor is evident in many of the people I profiled, even the bicycle messenger and the shoe-shine man. But there is a long list of workers who find it extremely difficult to achieve a well-adjusted life: underpaid, abused immigrants who make our garments, serve us dim sum, wash our dishes, and clean our cars; former welfare recipients forced to take jobs that endanger their health, and African Americans who suffer racial slights on a regular basis. In this last category, one worker in particular sticks out in my mind. He was a civil servant so distressed by his job that I feared for his health; and when I called months later with follow-up questions, he was in the hospital with severe hypertension. Weeks later still, he was back on the job, doing the best he could.

Someone whose opinion I value expressed concern that a disproportionate number—all, actually—of the people included in a section I call "The Fringe-Dwellers" are from racial minorities. That reader also believed that too many of the most highly paid workers are white. She was genuinely upset by this polarity and asked whether I had intended it to be this way, to which I replied no. At least not consciously. The whole question of race and ethnicity is a tricky one. Suffice it to say that I do see the city in tangibly racial terms. The broad neighborhood where I live in central Brooklyn is almost exclusively black, and it never ceases to amaze me how racially homogeneous other neighborhoods of the city are as well, how certain areas—Park Slope, Brooklyn Heights, Greenwich Village, and the Upper East and West Sides—remain overwhelmingly white and relatively affluent. Go into the jails, on the other hand (as a visitor, assuming you have the choice), and you will find them filled to overflowing with Blacks and Latinos, the very same groups you'll find at the city's homeless shelters. Given this, and the persistently high unemployment among Black and Latino youth, I don't think it should be terribly surprising to find racial clustering at the ends of the income spectrum, in this book or in anything else that reflects life in New York City.

My friend Ed's mother died weeks ago, and he's been looking for a new position in marketing, which I'm sure he'll get because he's one of the brightest people I know. A serious music buff, Ed called to ask if I still had an old Missa Luba album, cut in the 1960s by a Congolese Catholic choral group. In my basement I found the recording, which had fading liner notes by, of all people, Studs Terkel, author of the classic book *Working*. People whom I had approached about their jobs would often smile and ask if I was planning a reprise of Terkel's literary feat. My answer was always some variation of this: that in our verbal and visual portrait of the most ethnically diverse workforce in the world, Ozier and I were taking a different road to a similar place. We believe it's a place that will engage and inform a wide variety of readers.

ACKNOWLEDGMENTS

One Hundred Jobs shares with Studs Terkel's book *Working* a very important link, in the person of The New Press director André Schiffrin. It was André Schiffrin who came up with the idea for *One Hundred Jobs*, and it was the same André Schiffrin who inspired Terkel to do *Working* three decades ago. Ozier and I are happy to have been integral parts of this recent book, and we want to thank André and the late Joe Wood for together conceptualizing something so different and so interesting.

I want to acknowledge now the help of my wife Marilyn, who was my informal copyreader and counselor through the long process of writing and editing. Our son Damani inspired me during this time, as he entered the world of work and tried mightily and honestly to find his niche. My mother Marian was, well, always there. I also need to thank here a young journalist named Samy-Leigh Webster-Woog, to whom I turned in a pinch for time. For pay hardly equal to his talent, Samy interviewed some of the people in the book. (I made follow-up calls and wrote the text.) Two other reporters, Dylan Foley and Matthew Sweeney, also did interviews, so that all together I had such assistance on about twenty of the one hundred pieces. Thank you, Samy, Dylan, and Matt.

At The New Press, associate director Diane Wachtell was a strong and calming presence toward the end, stepping in to assist me after the untimely death of Joe Wood. By her side, doing the unnerving work of reconciling verb tenses in one hundred disparate stories, was copy editor Lydia Weaver. Editorial assistant Barbara Chuang served as my point of contact and fountain of information on deadlines and other critical matters. Managing editor Leda Scheintaub coaxed and chided as the time approached for the production train to leave.

Last but not least is Les, who would be Les Payne, assistant managing editor of *Newsday* and a person to whom I and a long list of others, among them Joe Wood, have turned for advice over the years, including on this book. The train transporting *One Hundred Jobs* has finally come and gone. I am on that train, looking back and waving in gratitude.

I. THE SELF-EMPLOYED

1. MAGICIAN

Salary: Upwards of $30,000 a year	**Experience or Requirements:** Lots of practice
Hours: Often 12 hours a day	**Use computer:** Yes, to keep records
Benefits: Health, self-provided	**Workplace:** Home, stages, and convention halls
Union: Yes	**Risks:** None, except embarrassment at failed tricks

To George Schindler, magic is not so much about fooling people as about entertaining. "You want to fool people, you go into politics," he says.

For more than a quarter of a century—after a career in the corporate world—Schindler has been realizing his childhood fantasy of doing magic professionally. He specializes in making things appear, disappear, or multiply in his hands or in the hands of spectators—sponge balls, coins, or cards. "It's called 'misdirection,' getting people to look someplace while your hand is doing something else."

As he is being interviewed, he is preparing to do "walk-around" tricks for a small private group. For such shows, professional magicians generally receive a basic fee of $350, plus $150 an hour, sometimes working up to three hours.

Occasionally Schindler will do trade shows, where his main task is to help sell a product. "The companies hire me to stop traffic, much like a barker used to do in a circus. I stop people and demonstrate a product or talk about it, in the context of doing magic. But if they leave and they don't know the name of the product, I've failed."

After years in the illusions business—and a 1992–93 stint as president of the Society of American Magicians—he has many contacts who help him out. And he returns the favor. "I have a magician friend with a summer camp. He had 150 kids. One by one, I taught 150 kids how to make a ball disappear."

In addition to performing, Schindler has written eight books about magic, including *Magic with Cards, Magic with Everyday Objects*, and *Ventriloquism! Magic with Your Voice*: "I get a nice little royalty check every once in a while." He also sells ventriloquist dolls and other equipment. Schindler says that a competent full-time magician can earn at least $30,000 a year, and that someone with his extensive background might even make in the low six figures, although he wouldn't reveal his income.

In his early teens, Schindler dreamed about doing tricks in front of a crowd, or being in some form of entertainment. He tried his hand for a while at comedy, but "fell on my face."

Then he slowly got sucked into the corporate world, eventually becoming vice president of an electronics marketing company. It wasn't until 1973 that he decided to submit to his inner desire and go into magic fulltime. "I had stock in the electronics company. I sold it, bought a new station wagon, and went out on the road. I was traveling the country, sawing people in half in department stores…"

Back in Brooklyn, he set up shop at home, where these days he practices, spends time on the phone drumming up business, and uses a computer to keep track of appointments and billings. He maintains liability insurance through the Magicians Society, and is a member of the Screen Actors Guild and the American Guild of Variety Artists. His wife Nina is his assistant at home and at his shows. "Sometimes we rehearse in the living room," he says. And after the performances, "The most fun we have is talking about the things that went wrong."

2. MASSAGE THERAPIST

Salary: Approximately $30,000 a year   **Experience or Requirements:** 1,000 hours of study
Hours: About 35 hours a week   **Use computer:** No
Benefits: None   **Workplace:** Small room
Union: No   **Risks:** Repetitive stress injury (RSI)

Three days a week, Anthony LaCagnina works at the New York Health and Racquet Club in Manhattan, where he thumps, rubs, and pounds the bodies of joggers and other hour-a-day athletes. "These people look on me like I can walk on water," he says, smiling momentarily.

LaCagnina also works one day a week out of a chiropractor's office in Queens, where he treats people who've been injured, often in car accidents. "Some people are so wracked with pain," he says, "it makes you think twice about driving a car."

A self-described nontraditionalist, he especially likes a technique called Reiki, in which the practitioner uses the warmth of his hands to help clients deal with their pain. "I place my hands on. And just the heat of my hands changes their pain threshold, and with that they're able to take some light massage work, to get some circulation and lymphatic fluid moving."

He calls this the "extremely rewarding" part of being a massage therapist, when his patients are visibly more relaxed and speak of release from pain. Some are enthusiastically grateful.

But increasingly the forty-one-year-old LaCagnina has been thinking about getting out of the massage therapy business. For one thing, he's been feeling the pains of repetitive stress injury. The intense, shooting sensation comes from hours and hours of deep massaging. Occasionally his hands hurt so much that they get numb, and he has to use his elbows or his forearms to continue massaging his clients. Other times, "I pull back for a while." He waits, rests a moment, massages his hands, and then continues.

Beyond that, he believes the thousands of dollars that he has spent over the years learning to become a certified massage therapist may not be giving him the status he expected. He wearies of people who equate him with the masseuses who advertise as therapists in the yellow pages but who are really selling sex. "I'm getting out of the yellow pages," he says with

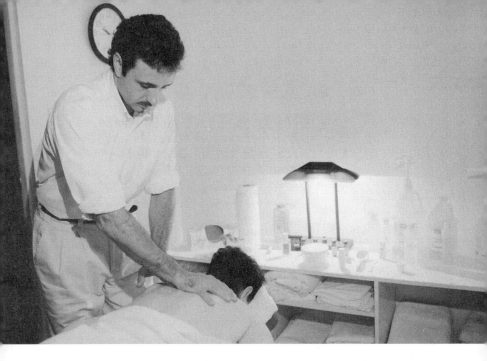

irritation. "You get a couple of kinds of calls. You get somebody who you could tell started his own treatment before he got on the phone....the kind who is 'getting off' on talking to a stranger."

Although massage therapists have to be certified by the state, there's no real policing of the industry, LaCagnina says. "Let's face it. With the crime in the city, they're gonna go after unlicensed massage therapists?"

He originally became a massage therapist because he enjoyed helping people feel good, and he thought it might be nice to make a living doing it. So he enrolled in a 1,000-hour course that cost about $10,000, studying anatomy and massage techniques, and finally obtained his New York State certificate in massage therapy. When he lost his job at an airport bar in the mid-1990s, he decided to go full-time into the body-rubbing business.

But now he's not sure he'll stay with it. "It's not an easy living. You're working for yourself. You've got responsibility for health insurance. There's no 401 K. No stock options. All of the things you have with a company, you don't have. And you have to rely on people being in so much pain or having enough money that they will pay you. I've been doing it full-time for a couple of years, and I think if somebody offered me a job out of the massage field and it was nine-to-five and it had good benefits and it was something I liked, I think I would take it."

3. MASTER SHOE TECHNICIAN
(SHOE-SHINE MAN)

Income: $7,800 a year, sometimes more, sometimes less

Hours: 8 a day, 6 days a week

Benefits: None

Union: No

Experience or Requirements: On the job

Use computer: No

Workplace: A high chair

Risks: Back strain

"I didn't have no work. I needed some work, and I got interested in shining shoes. It's not for everybody. It grows on you." Thirty-eight-year-old Ricky Pemberton has been doing it now for twelve years and is established enough to have a business card ("Rick Shoe Shine…Clean Exotic Shoes & Boots"). "We shine the old way," he explains, "the way our ancestors shined. We put on two, three coats of polish. We stay with the shoe. We look at the shoe. See what it needs. If it's very dirty, we wash it off with water, or put the shoe wash on it, which is a conditioner and a wash."

Then he puts a coat of polish or cream on the shoe. "The kind of shoes we put cream on are the exotic shoes, alligator, ostrich, crocodile, snake, lizard, or eel. You got to use cream to get into it, like human flesh…"

After polishing and brushing and buffing—rough side of the rag first, the cotton side second—he is done. "It takes approximately ten to fifteen minutes to do a shoe properly," he says. "If someone does it in two minutes, they're doing *at* it. They're not doing it."

One guy was so happy with Pemberton's workmanship that he left a $100 tip. Then again, there was the fellow who tipped him a dime.

Pemberton charges $2 and up, the highest price being $15. "That's for what we call 'hooker boots' that go over your knee. You remember in the old days hookers wore boots that went up to their knees and wore hot pants?"

In a good week, he can make upwards of $300, mostly from November through April, because "that's when people come in with boots. In the summertime, people wear sandals and sneakers." Even then, however, he says he has to shell out more than $150 a week for rent, polish, and equipment.

Guys who shine shoes in midtown, such as those near Grand Central Station, can make several hundred more than he does, Pemberton says. But he likes being in Harlem.

Residing in a single-room-occupancy unit a short walk away, Pemberton knows almost everyone in the neighborhood. He shares the storefront space on Frederick Douglass Boulevard with a shoe repair shop and a tiny take-out food business. His space has several chairs with footrests, under which he keeps sixteen different brushes as well as tins of polish and bottles of water and dyes.

At over six feet, Pemberton has to bend over quite a bit in order to reach the shoe he is working on. "Once my back went out of whack," he says, and even today he experiences back pains.

He feels that he merits a title better than "bootblack" (what Pemberton calls "that old-fashioned term") or shoe-shine man, although he really doesn't mind either of them. What he hates is being called a "shoe-shine boy." The term he likes best is shoe technician. "'Master shoe technician.' Put that down," he says.

What he enjoys more than anything else about the shoe-shine business is the independence of being his own boss. That said, the public relations man in him rises to the fore, and he corrects himself. "Our boss," he offers with gentility, "is our customer."

4. DOG WALKER AND GROOMER

Salary: $50,000 to $60,000 a year

Hours: 10 to 12 a day, 6 days a week

Benefits: None

Union: No

Experience or Requirements: Dog grooming school

Use computer: Yes

Workplace: Home (hers and customers'), sidewalk curbs, fire hydrants

Risks: Wrist sprains, aggravation of allergies

Carol Sessler's day begins a bit before 8:00 A.M., when she rushes over to pick up her first client of the day. Recently it's been a friendly Doberman pinscher that Sessler takes for a stroll, a poop, and a pee.

Sessler walks between ten and fifteen pooches a day, along the streets of Manhattan and through Central Park, where she lets them exercise with other animals. She charges $12 for a half-hour, $20 for an hour. In the evenings she does grooming, carrying her foldable table to her customers' homes, where she shampoos, blow-dries, clips, and brushes the animals. For the grooming, she charges upwards of $50.

"I'm so fascinated by dogs, I'm so fascinated by their personalities," she says, "and each one of them I have a distinct relationship with. And you just can't be depressed. You just can't be depressed with this."

Caring for pets in Manhattan is a boutique industry, supported by owners financially able to give their animals the very best. Each day Sessler regularly sees about ten other people doing the same work in her immediate West Side neighborhood.

Sessler, who is forty-two years old, has a bachelor's degree in nutritional science. She once planned to have a career in acting, and she ran a graphics and resumé writing service out of her apartment. But after taking a seven-week course at the New York School of Dog Grooming, at a cost of $1,875, she began dedicating herself full-time to her business, Doggie TLC. She has been doing it for two-and-a-half years now. She would someday like to open a "comprehensive facility" for the care of pets and has been talking with potential investors.

Because she is asthmatic, a doctor advised Sessler to go into a different line of work. But she says she is determined to make it as a dog walker, groomer, and trainer. When she is washing and brushing her hairy clients, she wears a surgical mask to protect against outbreaks. She also takes anti-asthma medications.

The job can be physically challenging, even though the pets are friendly. Sessler has developed severe strain in her left wrist from walking larger dogs that playfully jerk the leash. Still, "the enjoyment I have on a daily basis outweighs the risks," she says.

It is an enjoyment that can be touchy-feely, as when owners pay her to massage their pets. "One of my clients, actually the Doberman owner, asked me if I would watch this video and learn how to massage the dog, because the dog was lame in one leg. What she wanted me to do was to come every day for a month or so and massage her dog." Sessler did that, and then began massaging other pets, including a cat that had fallen five stories out of a window.

A self-confessed workaholic, who is out there hustling every day but Sunday, Sessler believes she has finally found her calling. "At the time I was doing [the acting], I felt I had to be someone else to be successful, to make it.... That has never been an issue with this work. I get to be fully myself.... It's not brain surgery, but it's rewarding beyond words."

5. FUNERAL DIRECTOR

Salary: About $160,000 a year, together with co-owner, his mother

Hours: 12 a day, 7 days a week

Benefits: Health, vacation

Union: No

Experience or Requirements: A year of funeral directors' school, a year of apprenticeship, and two state exams

Use computer: Yes

Workplace: Funeral parlor, cemeteries

Risks: None reported

Two Buddhist monks are beating their sticks rhythmically and chanting, as the bereaved family stands around in a semicircle, all of them dressed in black. In front of them is the open casket of the man whose death they have gathered to mourn.

Down the hallway, about thirty feet away, Joseph Yick is busy in his tiny front office, using special software to type up Chinese characters that are to be placed on the urn of a person who has recently been cremated. Yick, co-owner and director of the Wah Wing Sang Funeral Home in Chinatown, is a member of a profession that has been maligned in books and investigative news stories about the high cost of dying.

The cheapest method of sending off a loved one would be to have the body taken from the place of death to a crematorium, without a funeral service. That would cost about $500, Yick says. But for a typical funeral, Wah Wing Sang charges between $7,000 and $8,000, a range that Yick acknowledges is higher than the local average. The reason, he says, is that Chinese immigrants tend to purchase vaults, the often-pricey protective coverings of wood, steel, or concrete into which caskets are placed.

"The Chinese believe that they have to protect the person that passed away as much as possible," says Yick, age thirty-nine. "Whereas some funeral homes have to push and sell, I just sit back because that tradition has been followed for so many years." By law, Yick says, funeral directors have to tell customers that it is not necessary to buy vaults, or even to have bodies embalmed, but the vast majority of his customers do both anyway.

As Yick speaks, the family that had been standing with the monks is now performing a traditional ritual of tossing fake dollar bills, called "Hell

Notes," into a bucket with flames. "That represents money for the decedent to use in the afterlife," Yick says.

Wah Wing Sang, meaning "The Chinese Community Living Forever," handles about 300 funerals a year. Yick and his mother Martha, who these days is only there part-time, supervise a staff of six employees. Typically, a family will call the parlor immediately after a death, or just walk in. The first order of business is explaining costs and funeral options. Often the families need assistance in filing demands for payments from life insurance companies. As do many other funeral homes, Wah Wing Sang contracts out the embalming of the bodies.

Yick considers the funeral-directing business to be, before all else, a "people job." He says he tries to remain emotionally detached so he can do his job well. But he often feels special pain and sorrow, for example, when there are multiple deaths in a single family or when the deceased persons are very young. He cited a time when he handled the funerals of three young brothers who drowned while swimming together.

Ying commutes from his home in New Jersey and parks right in front of the parlor. "The local police know who I am, and know I have a business to run," so they do not ticket him.

After giving up a career in engineering, Yick attended the American Academy McAllister Institute of Funeral Service in Manhattan, and in 1989 joined the family business that his parents started in 1954. The long hours are the most difficult part of the job, and even at the young age of thirty-nine he finds himself looking forward to retirement in fifteen years or so.

6. EMBALMER

Salary: About $55,000 a year, net

Hours: 16 a day, Monday through Saturday, and 8 hours on Sunday

Benefits: Health, pension, vacation

Union: Yes

Experience or Requirements: Associate's degree in mortuary science, state funeral directors' license

Use computer: Yes

Workplace: Office and adjacent room with dead bodies

Risks: Back strain and hepatitis

Six times a day, on the average, Rocco Paccione gets a call to go to a house, nursing home, or hospital to pick up a dead body to prepare. "Unlike most other jobs, we can't say I'll do it tomorrow," says Paccione, age forty, owner of Paccione Funeral Services in the Park Slope section of Brooklyn.

Some funeral homes do the work themselves, but a large number prefer to farm out the heavy lifting and the bloody preparation work to journeymen embalmers like Paccione. There are perhaps two dozen "trade embalmers" who pick up, transport, and "prepare" dead bodies for funeral homes in New York City, Paccione says.

"Preparing bodies" is a euphemism for the process of making an incision in the veins and arteries of a dead person, draining the blood, and then filling the corpse with a formaldehyde preservative. Paccione rotates such duties with six employees, all of them men and all licensed embalmers. The work is done in a basement "operatory," a 33-by-11-foot room with five embalming tables and a machine called an "air handler" that recycles the air every four minutes.

"We have to keep the formaldehyde [fumes] below a certain level," Paccione says, referring to stringent guidelines established by the U.S. Occupational Safety and Health Administration. The embalmers wear masks, gloves, and bodysuits to protect them from possibly contagious viruses.

The embalming process normally takes about an hour and a half. But sometimes it runs several hours. The longer operations are required when a body has already been cut open—perhaps for an autopsy or the removal of a donated organ—and the embalmers must stitch it back up with needles and waxed linen thread. The embalmers then transport the body to the funeral home, dress it, and put makeup on it.

Critics have alleged that embalming is unnecessary, but Paccione argues that embalming returns the body to an approximation of its "natural" appearance and helps family and friends cope with their loss in an emotionally healthy way.

Paccione's spacious office is right outside the operatory. He rents the whole area from Duffy's Funeral Home. As he works at his desk, behind which sit a computer and a fax machine, Paccione often listens to light jazz on an Aiwa stereo player. There is also a television and a refrigerator in the office. On the day he was interviewed, a copy of a book, *Just a Breath Away*, was nestled among the files and papers. The book, he says, was written by a friend, the Rev. Edward Tabbitas. "He's of a mind that death is not final, and so am I," Paccione says.

As a journeyman embalmer, Paccione is a member of Local 813 of the Teamsters, through which he gets his health insurance and pension. But all embalmers are also licensed funeral directors, and as a funeral director, he is also a member of the National Funeral Directors Association. In addition to the embalming business in Brooklyn, Paccione says he owns a small funeral home in Staten Island that represents a minor portion of his annual income.

Salaried embalmers, such as those working for Paccione, earn between $450 and $900 a week. While there is always the risk of back injury from lifting bodies and of contagion from exposure to viruses, neither he nor his employees have suffered serious injuries or illnesses. In the embalming business, Paccione says, "You develop a much greater appreciation for life itself, the good and the bad, the ups and downs, and you realize that not everyone is dealt a fair hand, and you thank God and chalk it up to a good day."

7. FLOWER SHOP OWNER

Salary: Approximately $50,000 a year, net

Hours: 12 a day, 6 days a week

Benefits: Health, self-provided

Union: Yes

Experience or Requirements: Worked in flower shops in his youth

Use computer: No

Workplace: 1,100 square feet of plants and flowers off a busy commercial street

Risks: Getting tagged by the IRS

There are several hundred plants and thirty varieties of flowers in Stanley Ligon's shop. He likes touching them and arranging them, and using his big reference book *The Exotica* to look up their origins, significance, and etymology. "It's soothing to work around plants all day. It's constant therapy," says Ligon, who is thirty-five years old. "It's hassle-free. Nine out of ten people coming into a florist, they're going to buy. It's just helping them decide what they're going to get.... Very rarely do people walk in mean and nasty to a flower shop. You get to interact with nice people."

For all his love of flora and flower-loving people, Ligon freely concedes that he is in the business to make money. He enjoys purchasing good art and taking vacations, which leads him to a soul-baring confession: To pay his bills and his two part-time employees, Ligon has from time to time held back on tax payments to Uncle Sam.

But the devil has taken his due in the form of immense fines and interest. About six months before he was interviewed, Ligon says, he received a notice that he owed the federal government $19,000, about half of which was interest and penalties from payments he had missed two years previously. Although he grosses about $160,000, he says that most of it goes toward rent, inventory, salaries, and other expenses, and he is trying through his accountant to come to terms with the IRS. "I have lived and learned, and I am trying to do things as much as possible by the book as I can," he says.

A customer, apparently a friend of a friend from his old neighborhood in Brooklyn, approaches him as he is on the telephone. Cradling the receiver, Ligon turns to him. "One red rose? Two dollars. Normally three dollars, but since you're 'family,' I'll take the dollar off." The single rose, he explains, is of a type called Black Magic. "It has a velvet texture," he says. "At any given time we have anywhere between five and seven different varieties of roses." Fire and Ice, Raphaela, Nicole, Black Magic, Konfetti, and Skyline are among the most popular.

Located on a commercial strip straddling two fairly well-to-do residential neighborhoods, Park Slope and Prospect Heights, Ligon's shop, called Floral Gallery, is near several other florists with whom he competes. He says that, in his line of work especially, competition is a good thing. "Having four or five florists within a ten-block radius is good. It keeps us all on our toes. It puts it in people's minds, 'I know I'll find a florist on Flatbush Avenue.'" One-third of his annual sales are to institutions such as churches.

Having grown up in Apopka, Florida, where plants were a staple, Ligon feels he has a natural affinity for his work. But he also owns a cleaning business that employs several people, and he wants to open a restaurant—all with the intention of making money. "I do love flowers, but that's not only why I'm in it. I think it's a great opportunity to earn an easy income."

8. DAY-CARE PROVIDER

Salary: $45,000 to $50,000 a year, gross
Hours: 12 a day, Monday through Friday
Benefits: Health, self-provided
Union: No
Experience or Requirements: License from the state department of health
Use computer: Frequently
Workplace: Home
Risks: Colds

It is evening, and the ten or so children in Martha Taylor's brownstone home are starting to get a little restless. "No kissing!" bellows one of the adults. "Jillian, I want your shoes on your feet!" says another. One little fellow ostentatiously pokes a pacifier out of his mouth. Another dashes around in happy pursuit of no one. "This is the most excitable time for them because parents are coming," explains Taylor patiently. Taylor, age forty-four, owns and operates the "Wonderful World of Kids" day-care center located on the first floor of her three-story brownstone in the Bedford-Stuyvesant section of Brooklyn. The front room has Disney characters on the walls and is brightly colored. In that room Taylor keeps a computer and a library of software programs to teach and entertain her charges.

Taylor's day starts at about 5:15 A.M. when the first of the children, who are ages one through five, begin arriving. Taylor serves breakfast to all of them. Then the day really starts. "We use the computer in the morning, when they're more alert," she says. "They spell and count. Three-year-olds can count to fifty." Taylor often takes them to the nearby playground or on walks through the neighborhood. Back at the house, they snack and play. Working with Taylor are a young woman she hired and a worker provided through the Work Experience Program. WEP is the city program requiring people on welfare to work in some capacity for their paychecks.

At the Wonderful World of Kids, television is allowed, "but only Channel 13," the local public educational station. Naptime is after lunch, generally between 1:00 P.M. and 3:00 P.M.

Dealing with the city bureaucracy, which issues licenses for day-care providers, can be a headache. Toward the end of 1998, health department inspectors told her the center did not have two front means of egress and threatened to shut her down. She argued that she *did* have two exits, one on the first floor and one on the second floor. With the help of an elected official, she got her new certification.

Taylor says there is a plethora of people (many of them immigrants) doing home-based day-care in New York City, but most of them don't know how to run it as a business. Taylor is president of a neighborhood group (Child Care Providers) that shares information and organizes seminars regarding day-care.

Taylor says the day-care center is tiring but also potentially lucrative. Parents pay about $125 a week for five days a week, ten hours a day. "Most of my parents are police officers," she says. "One works for Bell Atlantic. One is a nurse." She expects her business to grow. "I know some making at least $100,000 a year doing this," she says.

Although she started the business just three years ago, it is something she had on her mind for many years, even when she was a banker. For twenty-two years at a large bank, Taylor climbed the corporate ladder. She started out as a typist, then became an assistant treasurer, then an assistant vice president. But she grew weary of the need to smile when she didn't feel like smiling. When the bank downsized, she took the offered financial package and decided to start the Wonderful World of Kids. "This is something I've always wanted to do, she says." Still, it's a job, and she makes that clear to the parents. She wants them to come on time for their kids. "You have to embarrass them," she says. "I tell them, Just like you want to leave your work on time, I want to leave mine on time, too."

9. KARAOKE HOST

Salary: Roughly $50,000 a year, net, for self and partner	**Experience or Requirements:** Singing, ability to work with digital technology
Hours: Nights, generally	**Use computer:** Yes
Benefits: Health, pension, self-provided	**Workplace:** Karaoke clubs
Union: No	**Risks:** Drunk patrons

"All right, ladies and gentlemen, let's hear it for...!" Russell Targove whips up the crowd, encouraging them to applaud for the nervous soul who's about to sing an oldie-but-goodie. At age twenty-eight, Targove is a karaoke host. He puts on customized musical shows, earning about $1,500 for weddings or bar mitzvahs, a bit less for restaurant appearances, and still less for children's birthday parties.

Karaoke, with roots in Japan, is the craft of providing disk-jockey skills and digitized background music for people as they croon into a microphone, finding a few minutes of glory as singers of their favorite tunes. For the performances he organizes, Targove brings CDs and laser disks of more than 4,000 songs "from the 1930s to the present." Thanks to new computer technology, he can locate any request in a matter of seconds.

Targove himself got hooked on the concept after witnessing a performance at a favorite Filipino restaurant ten years ago. The host at the Filipino restaurant used a simple cassette, but the underlying concept was engraved on Targove's mind. Targove considers it his job to make the performers, and by extension the whole audience, feel the excitement of a live performance. He makes sure the music is in the right key and at the right volume, with just the right bass and treble. He massages tender egos. Acting as emcee, he leads the cheering after the song is completed, and he sometimes simply takes the microphone himself and waltzes along the floor, singing as the audience listens, eats, and drinks.

The hardest part of Targove's job is dealing with drunks. Once, a man, fortified by a few drinks and apparently thinking he could do better, tried to wrestle the microphone from a performer. Liquor is, quite simply, one of the hazards of the trade. "A lot of people got turned off from karaoke because it

was hokey," Targove says, and because many people were "basically getting drunk and making fools of themselves." But he's sticking with it.

For the past two years Targove has had a partner, singer Ebony Diaz. Sometimes Diaz manages a show on her own while Targove works another location. Occasionally, they hire subcontractors as singers and engineers. Targove says he has been putting on an average of 300 shows annually for the past five years, grossing as much as $100,000 a year. He keeps expenses low by operating out of a modest apartment in Long Island City.

Targove pays for health insurance for himself and Diaz, and has enough left over for retirement investments, he says. About $10,000 of his income goes toward various insurance policies—theft and liability, in addition to health—and another $40,000 or so goes for other expenses, including equipment and salaries of the singers and engineers he contracts with. And even the approximately $50,000 that is his profit he plows back into new supplies and into marketing efforts. Both he and Diaz feel they are doing what comes naturally to them. "In high school I was in a fifties-type a cappella, doo-wop group," Targove says. "Karaoke is the vehicle that allows me to do what I do best—perform." And Diaz, like Targove, treasures her sense of freedom. "I've always been a singer. I've never had a nine-to-five," she says.

10. COSTUME MAKER

Salary: About $30,000 a year gross, with most going toward expenses

Hours: Sometimes 16 a day, 7 days a week, in heaviest season

Benefits: None

Union: No

Experience or Requirements: Associate's degree in art

Workplace: A shop

Risks: Rent increases

From the outside, Claude Jeffers's storefront business looks like a museum. Which is the way he likes it, because Jeffers wants people to feel free to walk in and see the colorful, peacock-like costumes he designs for the West Indian Day Parade, which draws two million people to his neighborhood in Brooklyn on Labor Day.

He sits for hours on end drawing patterns or stringing beads. Jeffers is busiest in the weeks before the Labor Day parade. The event, also known as "Jump Up" or "Mas," is the biggest source of his annual income. When he is not busy making ornate costumes for members of the dozens of bands that participate in the Brooklyn parade, he is fulfilling contracts for celebrations in other cities, such as the November carnival in Miami.

His creations range from simple elfin getups for children to sweeping, colorful headdresses to magnificent pieces that trail for yards, constructed from ostrich feathers, beads, and sequins. The most elaborate ones are for the kings and queens of the various societies that march in the parade. For a king or a queen costume, he charges between $3,000 to $5,000. He makes a total of about 900 costumes a year, and has lately started what he calls a "cottage industry" of costume dolls, a few of which he keeps in the front window as enticers. To further supplement his income, he also designs posters for various immigrant groups.

Known through the Caribbean community as Swami, Jeffers is fifty-one years old. He has sweet childhood memories of the lavish Trinidadian carnivals that set a standard for the Caribbean region. "The carnival in Trinidad had a big influence on my life. The whole country gets involved. And by being involved I always thought it was just something that everybody did. It seems like at carnival time everybody made a costume.

I didn't know costume making was a skill or a profession. But I came to America and I realized it's a skill."

Swami, who opened Swami Design in the mid-1990s, is a devotee of Rastafarianism, and like other Rastafarians he has a special reverence for Jamaican ganja, or marijuana. "I thank God for giving me the day, and I praise Him with the holy herb," he says. "I see religion in art and creativity."

Financially, Jeffers is still struggling. He grosses about $30,000 a year but says about three-quarters of that goes toward expenses, including about $1,200 a month in rent. But he would not work any other job and he would not live or work anyplace besides a mostly black neighborhood like his own Prospect Park/Lefferts Gardens. "The only time I'm not working is when I am sleeping," he says. "Even on the train I am thinking about designs."

11. ICE CREAM MAN

Salary: About $10,400 a year net
Hours: 12 a day, 7 days a week, in season
Benefits: None
Union: No

Experience or Requirements: Driver's license, licenses from consumer affairs and health departments
Use computer: No
Workplace: Neighborhoods of central Brooklyn
Risks: Holdups

Igenio de la Cruz sits silently in the driver's seat, leaning on the steering wheel. Above him is a console from which he can select any of thirty-two carousel-type tunes, all of them happy and bouncy. What, after all, could be happier than an ice cream truck on a hot day? But de la Cruz, age thirty, doesn't look particularly cheerful. During the summer and spring, when he rents his "Kool Man" truck, he works long days, every day of the week, and he says he's always tired.

De la Cruz picks up his truck from a company garage early in the morning, then cruises around central Brooklyn's black and Latino neighborhoods until someone waves him down. He pulls over, hoping to draw a crowd, and then he sits and waits with the engine idling. He looks over his invoices and changes the songs playing at the console. Manning the ice cream dispenser at the rear of the truck is a teenager he hired. The young man stands at the sales window, taking orders and preparing the cones, shakes, and splits that are the standard fare. De la Cruz needs the young man—who gets paid up to $35 a day, depending on how much ice cream he sells—because the black teenager speaks English, and de la Cruz is much more comfortable in Spanish. The young worker is quiet and businesslike. So is de la Cruz.

Quite a bit of calculating is involved in the Kool Man business. In addition to paying the young man, de la Cruz has to shell out $75 daily for the rental of the truck, plus more than $100 for syrups and packaged items like ice cream sandwiches. He buys milk on the street. On rainy days, knowing sales will be very low, the truck owner charges him half-price for the daily rental. All told, Cruz makes a profit of between $200 and $500 a week, with $200 being closer to the normal take. "I had a week when I had a loss."

One of his biggest fears is being held up. "One day I was selling, and a guy said, 'Give me an ice cream and the money.' But I hit the accelerator and fled," recalls de la Cruz. His brother also rents a Kool Man truck. "They robbed my brother three years ago. Four hundred dollars they took," he says.

During the winter and late fall, de la Cruz has to continue making money, so he shares a 1990 Ford Lincoln with a friend, and they take turns driving it as a taxicab. They split the car insurance (which in high-cost Brooklyn amounts to $3,000 every six months) and other expenses. With his cab, he makes a salary comparable to what he gets with the Kool Man truck. But he stresses that he could not do the taxi work year-round, because he would not get many calls during the summer.

The lack of health insurance is a continual preoccupation for de la Cruz, who has a wife who works as a waitress but is in poor health. When she has required regular visits to medical specialists in the past (such as for a bacterial infection that afflicted her), he has found it less costly to pay the $450 for a round-trip ticket to the Dominican Republic and have her take advantage of that country's cheaper medical services. If he can ever save enough money, de la Cruz would like to return to his native Dominican Republic to live. "It is much calmer there," he says. In the meantime, he says with resignation, "I am surviving."

12. OWNER OF TV REPAIR BUSINESS

Income: Several hundred thousand dollars a year, gross
Hours: Often 12 a day, six days a week
Benefits: Health, self-provided
Union: No

Experience or Requirements: On the job
Use computer: Heavily
Workplace: A storefront shop
Risks: Falling behind changes in the new technology

One by one, they have fallen off the radar screen. Rick Greengus is talking about the men and women—mostly men—who used to work in the television repair business. New technology has transformed the TV repair field and left many victims in its wake, he says.

In the old days, a person could open a little shop and, with the help of an easy-to-acquire manual, repair most appliances that came his way. No longer. "Now the service manuals are on disks. All of it is done through computer," says Greengus. "And the kicker is, if you're not authorized by the manufacturer to do warranty service, you can't get the information. That's why a lot of these independents are closing, like Avon up here." He nodded in the direction of a former competitor who he said folded just a couple of months before. "It's now survival of the strongest," Greengus says.

The thirty-one-year-old Greengus is the owner of Aid Audio and Television Service Corp., an appliance repair business on a busy commercial strip in the Flushing section of Queens. He took it over from his father. Nine repairmen work for Greengus, one of them an "old-timer" in his seventies who has been doing repair work for decades. The trend toward things digital is causing quite a bit of stress for veterans like that old-timer, Greengus says. Busy at their worktables, and apparently a bit taken aback at the request, neither the "old-timer" nor his colleagues wanted to be interviewed about their jobs.

Greengus says his workers regularly attend training seminars offered by manufacturers. The sessions are generally in the New York vicinity and do not require much expenditure. But they are necessary. "You can't learn this stuff on your own," he says.

When Greengus is not looking over the work of his employees, or in the back office going over the books, or inspecting a troublesome appliance, he deals with customers. One weekday finds him in a bitter argument with a man who claims that one of Greengus's employees had been rude on the phone. Greengus maintains that all of his employees are polite and tells the man it was reckless of him to make the accusation. After the man leaves, Greengus says it takes street smarts as well as book learning to run a business like his.

The salaries of Greengus's employees range from $500 to $800 per week. They work nine-hour days Monday through Friday, and about five hours on Saturday. There is no standard salary or benefit package for the workers. Some get paid vacations. "It's like anything else; you have to show me you're worthy of it," he says, referring to the benefits.

Each year Greengus pays, very roughly, $300,000 in salaries to his workers. Add to that, of course, the costs of equipment and rent and one can see that it takes diligence to turn a nice profit from the upwards of "several hundred thousand" a year he grosses.

But Greengus asserts he's doing quite well, thank you, and that his is one family enterprise that will survive the age of new technology.

13. CHRISTIAN SUPPLY STORE OWNER

Salary: About $36,000 net	**Experience or Requirements:** Was a postal
Hours: 13 a day, 6 days a week	clerk in South Korea
Benefits: None	**Use computer:** Yes
Union: No	**Workplace:** A huge storefront
	Risks: Fatigue

Won Hye Choi looks harried and sleepy as she wipes her brow, thinks distractedly for a moment, and then punches another sale into the register. She concedes that all she does in life is work, sleep, and, on Sundays, go to church. But she says she is very happy.

Choi, forty-five years old, owns and manages the Halleluyah Church Supply store in the Flushing section of Queens, where she sells Bibles and other religious items to a mostly Korean immigrant clientele. In contrast to the look of fatigue on Choi's face, the atmosphere pervading her large store is one of celestial serenity. Pop Christian hymns waft from a stereo as several young employees go blithely about their tasks, entering numbers into inventory books, stamping prices onto items, and helping customers.

"Whassup? I got some new CDs for you to check out," a twentyish sales clerk says to two young men who have just walked into the store. He points out a new CD by the all-men's Christian singing group, The Promise Keepers. The two young men look over some of the hundreds of compact disks that line the wall opposite the sales desk as they chat amiably with the clerk. A large number of the Korean immigrants who have been flocking to New York City (largely to the Flushing section of Queens) over the past two decades are Christians. And Choi has been helping them fill their need for spiritual uplift. "That is why I am happy," she says.

The most stressful part of her work is making sure that customers receive on schedule all the materials they have ordered. She spends hours on a computer checking book requests, mailing dates, and prices. Generally, she herself mails the materials to the clients. "At times, it is very difficult," she says. "Customers complain, and I must react. I try to give

response by face and try to be fair and loving. At times I send mail, but they don't get it. Or the price, they think, is different."

Before entering this line of business, Choi attended a theological school in Korea and worked in the post office. In 1982 she emigrated to New York, where "I sewed in a factory. I cut the thread and ironed." In addition to the Flushing religious store, she and her husband own a smaller one in Chicago. Her only vacation every year consists of a trip to Chicago to attend a three-day exhibition of religious supplies.

Choi is thin and sprightly. Asked if she exercises to relieve her body of the day's stresses, she responds, "Just work. No exercise. Just sleep." The stresses do sometimes seem overwhelming, she admits. Even during her thirty-minute drive from her home on Long Island, "I think about what we have to do today." She opens at 9:30 A.M. and closes at about 10:30 P.M.

During the workday she tries to pray, silently, as much as she can. "My mind is tired, I pray to God, and God takes care of my mind and my stress, too."

14. HAIR BRAIDER

Salary: $14,000 a year

Hours: Several to 12 a day, 5 days a week

Benefits: None

Union: No

Experience or Requirements: 1,000 hours of beauty school, written exam for state cosmetology license

Use computer: Yes

Workplace: Basement of home

Risks: Holdups

Ever since she was a kid, Renee Hall-Samuel has loved braiding hair. Now she does it as a job. Operating out of the basement of her mother's home, where she lives, Hall-Samuel has arranged folding chairs for her waiting clients. A solitary chair, the one for the woman whose hair she's working on, sits in the middle of the room. Along the walls are the obligatory mirrors, and in the hallway a water cooler. Welcome to More Better Braids.

Hall-Samuel fashions several types of braids for her clients, ranging from simple plaits to various types of "extensions." Some of the extensions require her to use a needle and thread to sew store-purchased human hair into the hair of her client, adding length and thickness to the customer's natural locks. Moving with dexterous speed, the twenty-eight-year-old Hall-Samuel can do basic braids in half an hour, and she charges $40 for these. The more elaborate extensions can take a whole day, up to eight hours, and can cost between $100 and $275. "Normally they come in here knowing what they want," she says of her clients. "They like the setting because it's not a busy salon." Saturdays are her busiest days, when often Hall-Samuel works from 10:00 A.M. to 10:00 P.M. On some slow weekdays she may have only one or two customers.

To become licensed as a beautician, Hall-Samuel took out a loan ten years ago and attended a school of hair design in downtown Brooklyn. She worked for a while in a salon, but now she prefers the independence of a home beauty shop. She has health insurance through her husband, a customer service representative at Consolidated Edison utility company.

In Brooklyn, or almost anywhere in the city for that matter, opening one's home to the public involves a certain risk, Hall-Samuel feels. Even so, she has recently begun advertising her business by handing out fliers in her neighborhood. She operates strictly by appointment. "Clients will ask if they can give out my number. You have to worry about it, but there's nothing you can do....[and] God has been good." No holdups or other such problems.

She has hopes of one day opening a full-fledged beauty salon in Manhattan, where she may do perms and shampooing and anything else an aspiring beauty queen might want for her head. But she has loved *braiding* ever since she was a child playing with baby dolls, and she finds it easy and even relaxing. "Some people think that braiding is tedious.... People ask 'Don't your fingers get tired?' My body may get tired. My back may get sore, but my fingers never get tired....It's just my preference. They come in with their hair clean, and they sit and I braid it."

15. SHOP OWNER TEACHING YOUTH TO REPAIR COMPUTERS

Salary: About $10,000 a year, on the average, after expenses	**Union:** No
	Experience or Requirements: Self-taught
Hours: 12 a day during week, 8 hours on Saturdays	**Use computer:** All day
	Workplace: A shop full of computers
Benefits: None	**Risks:** Low profit margins

Stephen Muñiz repairs and sells computers with the assistance of neighborhood youngsters who are unpaid but learning a valuable skill. His trainees are mostly from the surrounding neighborhood, which is heavily black and Latino, but they also come from other parts of the city. Over the past several years, the forty-three-year-old Muñiz says, he has worked with perhaps sixty such young people, including a couple with prison records. Sometimes they come as unpaid interns from nearby colleges; from time to time they walk in off the street, asking to tinker with the computers.

Custom Built Computers did about $110,000 worth of business in 1998, Muñiz says, but taxes, rent, equipment, and other expenses cut his profit down to $8,000. He has netted as much as $12,000 in a year, and he is hopeful of making much more, although getting rich isn't his goal. He believes that Custom Built Computers, which includes his main shop on Vanderbilt Avenue and another one about a quarter-mile away near downtown Brooklyn, will gross a million dollars annually in the near future.

Muñiz and his son are the only full-time employees of the company. Near the entrance to the storefront, two groups of trainees work. One is composed of several young men, the other, of two women. One of the women is Paula Powers. She had passed by the store three months ago and, noticing other young people inside, asked if she could come regularly, too. She and her partner Annette, who prefers to be identified only by her first name, have just finished working on a computer that Annette says is "unstable." "It would flicker," she says, referring to the monitor. "I took out the sound card and modem, and reseated them," which appeared to solve the problem.

Muñiz says he came up in life the hard way and wants to see the young people in his community succeed. And as for the accusation that he might be profiting from the free labor of the teens and young adults? "I could care less what a union might say," Muñiz responds. "They have no power over me. It's a free country. It's a free market. Besides, if they go into my bank account, they'll see how poor I am." The students are getting training that in just a month's time can land them jobs paying a decent salary, he says. For now, most of them are merely tinkering. "Only my top students work on units" that were brought in for repairs, he says. "The joy is when they go out and get jobs for $30,000 a year. That's a big motivator for me."

Muñiz started the business after turning his back on a marketing career with a top insurance company. Going on his own into the computer field was a difficult move, but it is one that gives him independence and a sense of doing good, says Muñiz, who is a devout member of a Pentecostal church. "We suffered a lot the first two years. It was a struggle just to get three dollars a day just to eat." But he is now seeing the light of day. Business is steadily improving. He has been running Custom Built Computers for nine years. "If you're constantly helping people, good things happen to you," he says. "All I ask is their loyalty, and they give it freely."

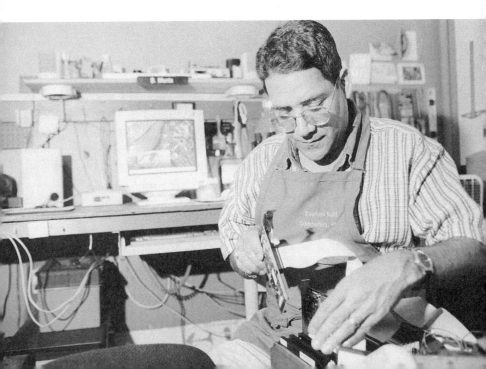

16. MARTIAL ARTS INSTRUCTOR

Income: Grosses more than $120,000 a year, but most of it goes toward expenses

Hours: 16 a day, 5 days a week, fewer hours on Saturdays and Sundays

Benefits: None

Union: No

Experience or Requirements: Black belt

Use computer: No

Workplace: A gym floor near Manhattan's financial district

Risks: Physical injuries

Eight punching bags hang from chains fastened to the high ceiling. Protective fighting masks and gloves dangle from the walls. The equipment will be used later. Class is about to begin. "Professor" David James faces the group of about fifteen students, mostly young men, and begins leading them in a round of jumping jacks. Thumping disco music booms from a stereo. After ten minutes, the warm-up exercise is clearly beginning to tire several students, one of whom stops and bends over in fatigue; another grimaces in apparent pain. They do a total of 500 jacks, and James jumps with them. Then they jog in place for several minutes, cooling down before the next set of drills.

James, who is forty years old, set up his martial arts school on Park Place near the financial district of Manhattan in 1992. He regularly keeps a roster of 100 to 150 students who each pay about $100 a month to be trained in Vee-Arnis-Jitsu, which is derived from the Filipino art of stick fighting. He also gets paid for overseeing belt-level tests at several affiliated schools started by former students of his. Receipts from his students add up to more than $10,000 a month, but "90 percent of that goes into rent" and other expenses. On weekdays he spends sixteen hours a day at his loftlike dojo (or martial arts studio). "I get in here at 7:15 A.M, and I do the cleaning and the maintenance of the place. I teach classes, group and private lessons through the day. I don't leave till twelve, twelve-thirty in the morning. I sleep about three to four hours a day." On weekends he often travels, teaching as a guest instructor at other schools.

He is bothered that martial arts instructors do not command more respect from the general public. "It's kind of like being a shoe-shine guy, I guess," he says. "It's not a job that's respected when you think of jobs. The picture that pops into your head is some guy in a basement teaching a couple of kids. They don't think of someone teaching martial arts as having a career. I have gotten more respect at social events if I tell people I'm a personal trainer, because Oprah has a personal trainer...so that has become a real job, a real career they know. Martial artists have not gotten to that point."

Finished with the jumping jacks, the class is ready to begin its *real* workout. Next, they are on the floor, kicking their legs in and out in an awkward-looking exercise. "Come on! Let's do it!" James shouts. "Oh, yeah, feels good!" Later in the evening class, which lasts from six o'clock until eight o'clock, the students take turns holding a protective shield while others punch or kick their midsections. "Get your ass kicking!" James yells.

James has been doing various forms of martial arts, including karate and jiu-jitsu, for more than twenty-five years. Many students cannot take the rigor of the classes and leave after several months, but others have stayed for the long haul, two, three years or more. They wear colored belts that show their rank, black, of course, being the ultimate achievement. "Out of 100 students, I'd say two stay long term, to make it to black belt," he says.

17. LANDLORD

Salary: $250–300,000 a year, net
Hours: Sometimes 1 a day, sometimes 15
Benefits: Health, self-provided
Union: No

Experience or Requirements: On the job
Use computer: Yes
Workplace: A little office with computer and fax machines, neighborhoods around Manhattan
Risks: Value will decline (very slight in Manhattan)

After years of making renovations to the three buildings he owns — and kicking out tenants who were there illegally — Nicholas Boeck figures he's gotten things down to a science. He often works full days, taking non-paying tenants to court, checking up on his superintendents, and collecting rent. But sometimes he hardly has to show up at all, if he doesn't want to. "I go through a period of like a week where I work fifteen hours a day. And then I'll go through a period of a week where I'll work one hour a day, which I love."

From his more than two dozen units, located in three buildings up and down the West Side of Manhattan, twenty-eight-year-old Boeck takes in a total of about $700,000 a year, although more than half of that goes to pay off mortgages, contractors, attorneys' fees, and other expenses. Together with his mother, with whom he bought the buildings, he nets about a quarter-million dollars annually. He adds, "And you don't have to spend that much money or put that much work into a lot of these buildings. Clean up the hallways, make sure the heat works, speak to the tenants like they're human beings, and that's the majority of the job." But getting to this point was not easy. "I went through hell the last five years to get to where I am today."

He began by buying properties from landlords who often were showing red ink. He got his initial cash from his mother, who sold her home in East Hampton when real estate was soaring in the 1980s. In deciding where to buy, he relied on a hunch that values would increase. Along the way, he forced out tenants who were staying — illegally, he says — on leases of previous residents. Annual income was modest, initially, he says. "For years, for two years, it was close to like $30,000."

He says he enjoys upgrading the apartments. "In a way I feel like this is almost an artistic job, because…if you have the time and the imagination, you can make each apartment very unique. That's what I try to do." After getting rid of the illegal tenants, some of whom were paying as little as a couple of hundred dollars a month, he was able to get substantially more rent for the units. Especially in Manhattan, many landlords used illicit tactics to force out low-paying tenants, including harassing them. Boeck says he does everything aboveboard and through the courts. He used a private investigator to confirm that the tenants whom he kicked out were not the people to whom the apartments were originally leased. "I try to do everything on the up-and-up because I like to sleep at night," he says.

Things have gotten so easy for Boeck that he's thinking of going into another field as the money rolls in from the rents and as he ponders the purchase of yet more buildings. "It's a fantastic business," he says of being a landlord, "and financially rewarding. People are made millionaires in the real estate business more than in any other business. It's great. Once you have a building up and running, operating, there's nothing really to it."

II. THE CIVIL SERVANTS

18. TRAFFIC ENFORCEMENT OFFICER

Salary: $23,000 a year **Experience or Requirements:** Written test

Hours: 8 a day, 5 days a week **Use computer:** No

Benefits: Health, pension, vacation **Workplace:** The streets of the city

Union: Yes **Risks:** Irate owners of ticketed vehicles

Once again, someone has pissed him off, and he storms along Second Avenue, throwing his hands in the air in frustration. "You can't come out here one day and have a peaceful day! Not one day!" thirty-year-old Anthony Jones says angrily. He is suited up in his white cap and blue traffic enforcement officer uniform. "These white people put it in their minds, 'Here is this black person issuing summonses,' and they've got a problem with it."

Minutes before, someone had publicly challenged him as he was writing a parking ticket in the East Village, near the Second Avenue Deli. Others joined in to support the person who was complaining. What bothers Jones is that people feel so free to argue with, and even yell at, traffic enforcement officers, even now that they have new, more official-looking blue uniforms, and their patch announces their ties to the New York City Police Department. The root of the hostility toward him and his colleagues, argues Jones, is that the agency is composed mostly of black and Latino agents. According to him, they are among the least respected of city employees, certainly of the uniformed services. "This particular agency is the lowest on the totem pole of all city agencies," he says. "In this neighborhood and with society, I'm shit."

Jones has been assaulted "quite a few times." When pressed for details on the most recent attack he says the offender was not white but black. Around Christmastime 1997, he had ticketed a car on Delancey Street, and the apparent owner of the vehicle "ran up behind me and assaulted me with a bottle." He chased the man, who jumped into the car and fled. "A female [police] officer saw it and they caught him....I had a slight contusion and stayed out for a day or two, and that was it."

Jones has been with Traffic Enforcement for ten years. Some agents have cushy assignments inspecting the agency's fleet or riding around on patrol checking for disabled vehicles. But Jones hasn't been able to land one of those duties full-time. He admits he doesn't like dealing with the public, and he feels pressured by the demands of the job. The agency expects its officers to meet an "office average" in giving out parking tickets, very roughly several dozen tickets a day. "If you don't meet the office average they put you on a 'low writer's program,'" he says, "and a supervisor goes out with you to try to determine what your deficiency is. I just got off the program." He had been on the program for four months.

Jones concedes that the paperwork on his job is simple. But there's so much that he hates about the job, including his commute. He takes a bus and then a train from his home in Queens to get to work in Manhattan. He shows up at 12:30 P.M. and is "mustered out" at about 1:00 P.M., taking a lunch hour between three o'clock and four o'clock, and two fifteen-minute breaks. He's off at eight-thirty. The routine is broken by confrontations with "sidewalk lawyers who want to tell you how to do your job, who get up in a crowd, like forming a lynch mob against me, like this guy here," he says, referring to the person who complained to him earlier. Noting that he has another fifteen years to go to retirement with a full pension, he says ruefully, "I don't know if I can make it that long."

19. LIBRARIAN

Salary: About $42,800 a year

Hours: 35 a week

Benefits: Health, pension, vacation

Union: Yes

Experience or Requirements: Degree in library science

Use computer: Yes, heavily

Workplace: Desk surrounded by books and computers

Risks: Changing technology, and too many questions

The main branch of the Staten Island public library opens at noon, but Dorothy Davison arrives two hours before that and begins stacking and arranging books. "I'm amazed at how people think we're at home with our feet up when the library is closed," she says later in the day, standing at her desk in the basement reference room of the library. She has to interrupt herself continuously to field nonstop phone calls and questions from library users. It is a holiday for the public schools, and that means a day full of children researching school assignments. About three dozen people are in her part of the library. In an hour's time, a third of the visitors have approached the fifty-one-year-old Davison for help in finding information or in handling one of the machines she has under her care. A recurring problem is confusion over the machine that dispenses the debit cards that are used to pay for photocopying and other services. A boy comes up to her. "Miss, the card doesn't want to come out of the copying machine."

"Did you press the red button?"

"Yes, but the card doesn't want to come out."

"Hmmm. Sounds really curious." Davison leaves her desk and solves the matter. "That's all we do all day," she says as she returns, referring to the machines: the regular photocopier, the eight microfilm machines, the microfilm copier, the computers for the CD-ROMs, the ones for the Internet, and on and on. The explosion of information resources, brought about by the computer revolution, has affected librarians more than most professionals, and Davison says that her job is "extremely" stressful. "If you're going to stay in this business, you have to evolve with it, and I'm not particularly afraid of new things," says Davison, who has a master's degree

in library science from Pratt Institute in Brooklyn. "But I know others who've dropped out. It definitely is a sea change."

Davison's desk is surrounded on three sides by reference books (more than 150 of them), pamphlets, a Dell computer, and a printer. A girl comes up to Davison with a question about how to get weather maps for a school project. A man wants to know about paper companies in Canada. And the phone rings, with a gentleman asking how to obtain stock prices from 1996.

Davison is a thirteen-year veteran of the library system and gets five weeks' vacation. She is a member of the union of city employees' District Council 37. Davison is by her own description a believer in order and symmetry, and while energetic, she has always been bookish. As an undergrad at Queens College she majored in medieval history. "This is not the kind of job you just drift into," she says of library work. Someone speaking with her notes the stereotypical finger-to-mouth image of the stern librarian, warning children to be silent. She replies: "We can't shush kids."

Then what do you do when they're noisy? she is asked.

"We shush them."

20. SANITATION WORKER

Salary: $44,000 base, $63,000 with overtime
Hours: 40 per week
Benefits: Health, pension
Union: Yes

Experience or Requirements: Civil service test, high school diploma or equivalent
Use computer: No
Workplace: The streets of the city
Risks: Back pain, cuts, noxious substances

Standing six feet tall and weighing over 300 pounds, Standish Benton doesn't complain about the lifting. It's what's inside the bags that worries him. "You don't know what the contents of a bag are—glass, fumes," says Benton, a city sanitation worker, or in the common parlance, a garbage man. "A sanitation worker died of lye or some kind of chemical in a bag...If there's a dead dog on the street, Sanitation has to pick it up. You just pray that you get through the day."

On a typical day, Benton shows up at his depot in lower Manhattan, signs in, and checks to see what his assignment for the tour is. On the day he was interviewed, he spent the morning collecting recyclable papers. For several hours of his eight-hour shift, Benton is on a truck, hanging on to it as it chugs along the streets, and getting off with his partner to pick up refuse, maybe twelve or thirteen tons of it in a tour. Much of the remaining time is spent transporting what was collected to any of a number of drop-off points around the city. Bundles are not supposed to weigh more than forty pounds, but Benton says that sometimes bigger things need to be removed from the street. "I picked up a dead horse once. And people booed us for some reason. The horse died of natural causes. We used a pickup truck with a hoist and took it to the Staten Island landfill."

Among the city's blue-collar workers and their children, sanitation has a reputation as one of the prized civil service jobs. Benton says he agrees wholeheartedly. "I was with transit as a cleaner, and with [the] parks [department] before that," says the forty-nine-year-old Benton, who walks every day to the depot from his apartment in the nearby Soho neighborhood of Manhattan. "This is the best job I've ever had with the city. This is a job where you know what you have to do and you do it. There's no stress."

The best part of the job, he says, is the strong union. "The union's a

good union, a powerful union. You have a problem, you go to the union. If I needed to go home in an emergency, I'd go to the supervisor and say, 'Can I go home?' and they'd usually resolve it then and there." With a plan similar to that of police and firefighters, sanitation workers can retire after twenty years at half of the average of the last three years' pay. "For the rest of your life," Benton says with a smile.

There are forty-two workers at Benton's depot, all of them men. The desirability of the job is confirmed by the many thousands of aspirants who show up to take the tests. "I know it's a good job when your people in suits ask you, 'When is the next test?'"

21. POSTAL WORKER

Salary: $37,800 a year base, about $42,000 with overtime
Hours: 40 a week
Benefits: Health, pension, vacation
Union: Yes

Experience or Requirements: Basic aptitude test, high school equivalency
Use computer: Yes
Workplace: Streets of northeast Queens
Risks: Back strain, dogs, peeping inspectors

George Martino is a careful, courteous, and very slow driver. After all, how fast can you go when you're getting out of your vehicle every two minutes? The fifty-one-year-old Martino drives a parcel truck for the U.S. Postal Service, picking up packages from 250 mail boxes throughout his route in northeast Queens. He logs about seventy miles a day, working from about ten in the morning until six in the evening. During that time, he chats very little with people, the way door-to-door mail deliverers do. Martino's district is composed mostly of single-family homes where almost everyone is out during the day. As a driver, he doesn't have to worry about vicious dogs that are the apprehension of many mail deliverers. Once during a stint as a deliverer, "A lady's dog broke away and came after me. I got my dog spray out, and it actually hit him and stopped him dead in his tracks. It was like pepper spray."

Martino, a thirty-two-year veteran, believes there are few workers who are under more surveillance than postal employees. In the office where the clerks and mail handlers are, postal inspectors keep a constant eye out for thievery. There are even peepholes through which the employees are watched.

The service keeps tabs on the two dozen drivers who work out of the Flushing office as well. Martino carries on his belt a small scanner that he uses every time he opens a mailbox. He activates the scanner and brushes it against an encoded strip on the side of the box. At the end of the day the information is downloaded into a computer. The most important thing it tells Martino's postal supervisors is that he was there. Second, it tells them what time he was there. He is allowed to be a little late on a pick-up, but he can't pick up early. If a box does not show up at all on the computer list, a driver is sent out immediately to make sure the mail was collected. "If it comes up a miss, it hurts the scores of our post office and it affects the pay of our bosses," Martino said. "We haven't missed a box in years."

Martino is in good physical condition, but says he is careful to lift packages properly so that he doesn't throw his back out. And the stuff they say about postal workers never missing their appointed rounds through rain and hail and so forth is true, largely. Martino once walked six miles through a snowstorm to get from his home in southern Queens to his job in the northern part of the borough. It took him two hours. But there have been times the city was so snowed under he was not able to get to work.

Whereas many people once looked down on postal work, these days tens of thousands take the tests and try to get any kind of position with the service. Starting salary is about $21,000, but veterans with eight or more years can earn twice that.

Martino, a member of the National Association of Letter Carriers, says that the real attraction is the job security, as well as the health coverage and pension plan. "There was a time when 70 percent (of new employees) would leave within a year and a half," he says, "but now they're beating down the door when they put the test out, because of the benefits."

22. DATA ENTRY CLERK

Salary: $26,000 a year	**Experience or Requirements:** Typing and
Hours: 35 per week	word processing at a special training program
Benefits: Health, pension, vacation	**Use computer:** Heavily
Union: Yes	**Workplace:** Small office with computer
	Risks: Repetitive stress injury (RSI)

Gina Long is at a computer for most of her seven-hour day at the men's homeless shelter on Bedford Avenue in Brooklyn. She types in information about clients and sometimes enjoys showing off her speed. "I'm screening the clients, getting personal data….I'll be doing it fast. I challenge myself. If he [the client] is brand-new, it might take me two minutes. That's why they like me, because I'm going real fast—name, Social Security, birthday, place of birth, parents' names, where staying before homeless, ethnic group, medical issues, addictions, psychiatric. You've got to know the codes. White, 1. Black, 2. Hispanic, 3." But then, Long says, she gets these pains. And when she gets them, they're a killer. "The worst pain is in my wrist. At any random moment I'll get a sharp pain in the arm, like someone hit me with something hard, or like someone poured liquid fire down my veins, straight up and down my arm."

Long, forty years old, has been working with the city Human Resources Administration, which oversees the city's homeless shelters, for almost ten years and is a member of District Council 37. "I wanted the benefits. I knew they had a union. And I thought in terms of retirement and security," she recalls of her decision to seek the job.

About three years ago, she says, she began to develop those occasional but sometimes excruciating pains up and down her right arm. She learned that the pain was due to something called repetitive stress injury, or RSI, which often affects people who use a computer for long hours or otherwise perform repetitive hand movements. A doctor wrote a note to her superiors saying she should not do computer work but something else, such as answering phones or filing. The supervisor was unsympathetic, according to Long. "She told me, 'Well, you only need one hand. If you can't use your

right, then use your left.' I just went back to my desk and I didn't do any work at first, but I felt obligated to do it, so I started working."

Soon, after reaching her ten-year mark on the job, she'll be eligible for the three-month leave permitted those who have RSI. Long finds herself looking forward to retirement. "In ten more years I can retire with a full pension, I think maybe three-quarters pay, but I'm not sure." But in the meantime, she thinks about a different type of job within the agency. She saw a notice about possible openings for counselors at a new city facility for troubled youngsters. The new place is in Brooklyn, where her current job is, and where she lives. "Possibly I could work there," she says. "But I don't know if I want to work with little criminals....Although at least that would take me off the computer." She admits to being a complainer, but believes her health is at issue. "I just may be one of those city workers that people talk about," she says, aware of the malingerer image of many civil servants. "But when I retire at age fifty, are my arms going to be numb?"

23. AIR TRAFFIC CONTROLLER

Salary: About $75,000 a year

Hours: 40 a week

Benefits: Health, pension, and $350,000 life insurance policy

Union: Yes

Experience or Requirements: Extremely difficult aptitude test and intense training course

Use computer: Yes

Workplace: Control room at or near airports

Risks: Stress of responsibility for lives lost due to error

From his perch at the LaGuardia airport control tower, Phil Fabricatore has the lives of hundreds of people in his hands. He determines altitude and distance from tiny blips on a radar screen, and makes quick decisions about the safety of planes landing or taking off. Add to that the strain of continually changing shifts—sometimes 7:00 A.M. to 3:00 P.M., other times 11:00 P.M. to 7:00 A.M.—and of the heavy air traffic at LaGuardia, which handles up to 2,000 flights a day, and the average person would feel intense stress. But other than the pack of cigarettes he smokes every day, Fabricatore doesn't show the tension. He was a smoker before he became an air traffic controller in 1989 and can't attribute the habit to the pressures of the job, he says. His duties are straightforward, as he sees them: "What we do is make sure planes don't hit. You take what would basically be chaos and make it organized....After a while you forget that there are people on the planes....They become like blips on a screen or tin cans running down the runway, or whatever."

If he is happy with his job—and he is—part of the satisfaction comes from the relatively good pay and benefits. A former construction contractor with no college degree, Fabricatore earns twice as much as a schoolteacher and has a pension plan allowing him to retire comfortably at age fifty-five. Controllers start out at about $40,000 and can make $100,000 or more, depending on seniority and the facility at which they work. Then there's the job security of being a federal employee. "It really is difficult to get fired from a civil service job at any level," he says. He is a member of the air traffic controllers union, called the National Air Traffic Controllers

Association, which has done well over the past decade protecting the rights of the current crop of traffic controllers.

Do "near misses," or the times when blips merge on the screen, rattle him? Certainly not to the point of ever having bad dreams. "I can't understand why, if you have nightmares, you'd ever come back to a job like this." He has experienced near misses, but never a crash. Fabricatore believes the real heroes are not the controllers but rather the investigators with the National Transportation Safety Board, who have to inspect the scenes of plane crashes, witnessing death and dismemberment periodically.

Things do get a little hairy inside the control tower, however. "We've seen actual physical contact between two people. When they're running eighty flights an hour, you get a little wound up...Arguments always happen, but stopping what you're doing and fighting? You're not allowed to hit anybody."

Recalling how he got the job, Fabricatore says, "I went through a physical and a psycho exam and a background check. Then we got a starting date for [training] school," which involved two months of intensive learning and "constant pressure to see how you performed."

Fabricatore drives to his Queens post from his home on Long Island. In the tower, he sometimes feels he's literally on top of the world. "You go up to the top of the tower. What do you see?" he asks rhetorically, referring to the panoramic view. "You see bridges, the city that's the greatest city in the world. You see the sky every day. Then you get to do something not everybody can do. Any time you talk to somebody about the job, the first thing out of their mouth is, 'I couldn't do that.'"

24. FIREFIGHTER

Salary: $62,000 a year, with overtime and benefits
Hours: About 44 a week, including overtime
Benefits: Health, pension, vacation
Union: Yes

Experience or Requirements: Written and physical tests, intensive training
Use computer: No
Workplace: Fire station, burning buildings
Risks: Heart disease, death by fire

"The New York City Fire Department is the ultimate," Randal Rodrigues says. "Nobody in the world is busier than the New York City Fire Department." Inside his firehouse, near the intersection of Lefferts Boulevard and 107th Avenue in Queens, the men rest, chat, do drills, and wait for the next alarm. They go out on an average of ten "runs" a day. Of those, maybe three or four are false alarms. The thought of death is often on their minds.

Once at the scene, "everybody goes into the fire, except the chauffeur, obviously," Rodrigues says. They have sixty-five pounds of gear on their backs, and their hearts pound in anticipation of what might lie ahead. Recalling his closest brush, Rodrigues says, "I had a leg fall through a stairway and the fire was below. The guys pulled me through."

Going into a burning building is like fighting close-up with a deadly enemy in bad weather and in the thick of night. Alluding to the movie *Backdraft*, which dramatized the lives of firefighters, Rodrigues says it's impossible to make a true-to-life movie about fires. "The movie would be black, because you couldn't see anything."

In the weeks before Rodrigues was interviewed, a spectacular fire took the lives of two city firefighters. "I happened to know one of the guys," he says.

Rodrigues, forty-one years old and a firefighter since 1989, loves the firefighter's schedule. "Most guys work twenty-four hours at a pop, which is really one of the main great things about this job—you can swap shifts," he says. That means that firefighters can have several consecutive days off to do other things, like work at a second or even a third job. Rodrigues, for instance, has what he describes as "a little DJ business" and he does some caddying. He is single, but most of his co-workers are "married guys who have homes and have mortgages" and "unfortunately…have to work second jobs." He and a large number of other firefighters live across the city line on Long Island, and drive to their jobs. "To come on the job, you get five bonus points if you live in the city," he says. "It's certainly a more affordable place, but do you want to live here? Most guys want to advance and they're living out on the Island." Firefighters start out at about $29,000 a year. But salary goes up with seniority, and there are plenty of opportunities for overtime. After five years, firefighters get five weeks' vacation. Like police officers, they can retire at half pay after twenty years on the job. And if a firefighter develops coronary problems, he can take advantage of the so-called "heart bill" and retire at three-quarters pay. The law was enacted years ago by the state and also applies to city cops. It was intended to recognize the special stresses of those jobs.

Rodrigues acknowledges that the fire department has remained a white male bastion over the years. He believes the vast majority of women simply don't have sufficient "upper body strength" for the job. The argument that women should be judged by different physical standards is "a bunch of crap," he says. He shrugs when asked why the police department has done a better job of attracting minorities. "I think it's much easier to become a cop," he says.

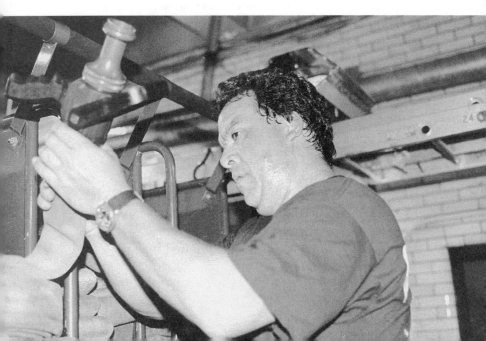

25. UNDERCOVER NARCOTICS COP

Salary: About $35,000 a year

Hours: 40 a week

Benefits: Health, pension, vacation

Union: Yes

Experience or Requirements: Two years of college, civil service exam

Use computer: No

Workplace: Streets and crack houses

Risks: Being shot by a drug dealer or another cop

Wearing dreadlocks and looking even younger than his twenty-nine years, the thin, smooth-faced black man has an easy time mixing with folks on the streets of southeast Queens. Five days a week, Paul Peterson (not his real name) goes out with his partner and a back-up team of six other police officers, trying to make drug busts. He and his partner are the "buy" part of the buy-and-bust team. While the six others wait in cars a distance away, Peterson or his buddy walks up to a group of guys suspected of selling narcotics. Peterson might strike up a conversation, or drop the name of a street person whose identity he learned through intelligence-gathering. Then he'll try to make a purchase. If he succeeds, one of two things will happen: either the back-up team will come and make an arrest, or the officers will note the information in their report and try to build a bigger case for a future bust.

Peterson finds the work exciting, but things get a little scary on occasion. "I had met a guy on the street and asked where I could get some crack. So I hung out with him, and he took me to a crack house," he recalls. One of the men inside the crack house beeped the dealer, who arrived by bicycle. But when opening the door for the dealer, the fellow noticed the car of Peterson's partner, and he shut and bolted the door, shouting that nobody should leave. "So I was stuck inside for about half an hour," Peterson says. "I was thinking he was probably thinking I was a cop. They sat there and they were smoking crack. I told them I had to go to the bathroom upstairs, and nobody was by the door, so I went out." A warrant was issued to search the location, and arrests were made a few weeks later.

Peterson's biggest complaint about the job is that the majority of undercover officers making drug purchases are black or Latino, while most of the investigators and supervisors are white. The investigators and supervisors acquire additional information about suspected drug dealers and locations, so that the undercover cops can know what they're getting into. "But the way I see a lot of the investigators and the bosses, they live on Long Island and they're not used to Brooklyn or the Bronx or whatever, and from what I've seen, a lot of them just don't know how to talk to people (and get information)." Peterson, who lives in Queens, says one of his biggest fears is that he may be shot by a policeman who doesn't know he's a cop. As an undercover officer, he carries a gun, but not his shield or identification.

When he is not on the street, Peterson spends up to several hours at the narcotics division's special two-story facility in southern Queens, filling out activity reports and planning future assignments. A four-year veteran, Peterson spent his first two years in uniform, making a total of about 200 arrests, he says, for crimes ranging from drug possession to assault. He is just weeks away from earning his gold detective's shield, which will increase his annual pay to about $45,000. Uniformed police officers earn between $32,000 and $41,000, reaching top pay after five years.

Police officers can retire at half pay after twenty years of service, and Peterson said he intends to do that after his twentieth year. In the meantime, all things considered, he enjoys undercover work. "It's not like the routine everyday things you do on patrol."

26. CORRECTIONS OFFICER

Salary: About $52,000 a year, including overtime	**Experience or Requirements:** Civil service exam, then training in self-defense, law, and firearms
Hours: 40 a week	**Use computer:** No
Benefits: Health, pension, vacation	**Workplace:** A jail
Union: Yes	**Risks:** Fights with inmates

Every workday, Karen Collins parks her car in the lot and then takes the special shuttle bus that transports her and other prison guards to various jails on Rikers Island. She is assigned to the Women's House of Detention. On the shuttle bus, she and her co-workers at the women's facility often laugh and joke. The others look haggard and resentful. The other officers, those assigned to the men's jails, occasionally complain that Collins and her buddies don't do real prison work, that they don't have to deal with violent, menacing prisoners. "Sometimes you can sit on the bus and look at the other officers and see the stress, see the tension," she says. "They don't see it as the same job, because we're just sitting and laughing. But I get the same salary and will probably live longer."

At the Women's House of Detention, Collins changes into her uniform and "stands for the roll call" at 0700 hours, or 7:00 A.M., with about sixty other officers on her 7:00 A.M. to 3:00 P.M. tour. Most of the officers with her are women. She rotates between two assignments. Some days she sits in a booth at the front entrance, wearing a bulletproof vest and a holstered nine-millimeter gun, inspecting the belongings of people coming into the building. Other times, she works in the "control building," where she hands out equipment such as keys, batons, and Mace to other officers working more closely with prisoners. While in the control building, Collins also operates the gates through which people pass to go from one part of the Women's House of Detention to another.

Prior to her current assignments, Collins worked for six years in the STEP program of the women's facility. In STEP, which stands for Self-Taught Empowerment and Pride, counselors build the self-esteem of the detainees and teach them social skills. Although there as a guard, she got to know some of the inmates fairly well and developed sympathy for them.

When she started as a corrections officer, immediately after her ten weeks at the training academy, Collins worked for three days in one of the men's facilities. "I remember walking up the corridor, another officer and myself ....The inmates were just screaming, 'Ms. Collins, we're gonna have you!' And that was a really scary feeling. I knew I just had to keep walking." On one of those three days, she recalls, eight alarms went off, meaning either that an officer was in trouble or that serious fighting had broken out. After the third day, in what Collins called "a godsend," she and her rookie partners were transferred to the Women's House of Detention. She was obviously relieved, but being a woman doesn't mean she won't ever get a dangerous post. "I heard of a female officer in a male facility. She attempted to take a phone from an inmate, and he literally opened her face with a shank," she says, referring to a makeshift jailhouse knife.

For the time being, she takes each workday as it comes, and mostly she appreciates them. Recently, she was the bikini-wearing Miss February in the corrections officers' "Hunks and Honeys" calendar. She's a nine-year veteran and has opted for the twenty-year plan, which means that in another eleven years, at the age of forty-two, she'll be able to retire with a full pension, about half her pay at that time. "Yeah, I like being a corrections officer, what I've done so far," says Collins, who lives in Queens, just a twenty-five-minute drive from her job. "I'm a people person."

27. U.S. NAVY RECRUITER

Salary: About $24,000 a year	**Experience or Requirements:** High
Hours: 8 a day, 5 days a week	school diploma, good health
Benefits: Health, housing, pension,	**Use computer:** Yes
vacation	**Workplace:** Office
Union: No	**Risks:** Short of war, not many

Juan A. Melendez tells the young men and women who come into his office that they can get theirs just as he got his. Looking sharp and confident in his dark Navy uniform, he describes himself as a regular guy from the Bronx who pulls in a total of $24,000 a year, not including benefits. The benefits are, by his description, unbeatable. They trip quickly from his mouth: housing, medical, education, and so on. A machinist's mate, first class in rank, Melendez was trained to work on fast-attack submarines, but he switched assignments and now works as a Navy recruiter in New York City. He concedes that the biggest lure into the armed forces today is not pure patriotism. "They're thinking about money, so it's all materialistic basically," says the thirty-three-year-old Melendez. The young men and women who come into his office are also turned on by the service because it's steady work. "You don't get laid off," he says, matter-of-factly.

The job of a recruiter can be frustrating, however. Most of the potential candidates are disqualified along the way. They often lack a high school diploma, have medical problems, or are in the country illegally. And that's before they get a chance to take the test. In general, "we have to interview thirty to get seven" who qualify and can enter the Navy, says Melendez.

Five Navy recruiters are assigned to his office on Flatbush Avenue in Brooklyn, and they try to recruit a total of about ten people a month. "I'd say I talk to about twenty to thirty people a day, including phone calls," says Melendez, sitting at a desk.

Relatively few people who walk into the office seem interested in dying for glory or in joining the elite gung-ho corps of sailors called the Seals. Those who want John Wayne-type action tend to go into the Marines. "We're different from the Marines and Army. Those are very physical. We're more on the mental aspect. We're more like technology people."

Which raises another troubling issue for Navy recruiters. The booming end-of-century American economy has created thousands of new jobs, and many of those jobs are of the low-end service or technical variety, attracting the very kind of young worker who might otherwise be interested in the Navy.

Melendez has been working as a recruiter for only a month. After his reassignment, he moved to an apartment in Brooklyn—for which he gets $926 a month in a housing allowance. He has put thirteen years of his life into the service, and is planning to retire with his pension when he's done twenty years. "But I may go past that," he says, referring to the twenty-year mark.

Melendez figures a significant number of those who inquire about the Navy are still lured, at least in part, by the storied glamor of being a sailor. "I'd say a third of the people like it as a way of getting dates or getting mates."

28. ZOOKEEPER

Salary: $37,500 a year base pay

Hours: 35 a week, plus some overtime

Benefits: Health, pension, vacation

Union: Yes

Experience or Requirements: Interest in animals

Use computer: Yes

Workplace: Outdoor and indoor cages

Risks: Bites from animals

Many young people romanticize the job of zookeeper. "Some of them just had a love of animals and thought it would satiate that need," says Roy Riffe. But then they find out what it's really like. "It's work," says Riffe, who's been a zookeeper for twenty-three years, the last ten with the Wildlife Conservation Society, which operates the zoo in Central Park. "It's raking leaves from the moat drain. It's cleaning up shit. People find out it's not as charming as it looks from the outside. There are only a few people like myself who come into the business and stay. You have to be driven by motivations other than money."

Riffe, age forty-four, doesn't romanticize the job, but his affection for animals, especially the pinnipeds, or fin-footed ones, helps make the drudgery tolerable. He comes in the morning, hoses down the cages, and tends the moat where the seals romp. He's the senior zookeeper, now technically called the senior wild animal keeper, and is in charge of all the outdoor animals at the park's zoo. Among the high points of the day for Riffe, who started out his career training dolphins and sea lions with a traveling show, are the three times a day he feeds the seals: 11:30 A.M., 2:00 P.M., and 4:00 P.M. Visitors gather around the moat as he and a junior keeper pull fish out of buckets, while the seals swim and clap and perform for their meals. On the day Riffe is found at Central Park, he is feeding Celia the seal, who extends her right fin first and then her left one. Then she barks. The crowd applauds. "It's a little presentation," Riffe says later, clad in his work boots and fatigue jacket.

With a bachelor's degree in wildlife sciences, which he recently obtained from Empire State College, Riffe knows his animals. Mishaps have been rare. But in a career as long as his, they are bound to happen at least once.

"About fifteen years ago I was bitten by a sea lion a couple of times," he says. "I was taking him right after he was weaned, and he was afraid of me. I got five stitches, and the scar is still there."

A lot has changed in the two decades since Riffe traveled with dolphins and entertained crowds around the country. Zookeepers these days use computers to keep information regarding their animals' health. His employer is a nonprofit organization, but since it receives money from the city, he is a member of Local 1501 of District Council 37. The Society paid for his studies at Empire State College. Riffe's base pay is $37,500, but he earns another $4,000 in overtime, and he gets five weeks' paid vacation and twelve holidays. A resident of the Washington Heights section of Manhattan and a regular rider of the subways, Riffe says he loves the park and loves the city. He considers himself the zoo's ambassador to the public. "I'm interacting with the public all day, talking to people. As far as I'm concerned, it doesn't get any better than this. I'm outside in the park, and I've got the New York skyline around me."

29. LIFEGUARD

Salary: $8.65 an hour ($21,590 annually)
Hours: 8 a day, 6 days a week during summers
Benefits: Health
Union: Yes

Experience or Requirements: Rigorous swim test, daily drills
Use computer: No
Workplace: A high chair on sand
Risks: Panicky nonswimmers in deep water

Here at Coney Island and at other public beaches, lifeguard work is a perennially popular summer job for youngsters who are strong swimmers.

Perched in his high chair on an overcast weekday, Anthony Brito surveys the scant crowd of beach-goers. He sports a beige New York City Lifeguard cap and an orange T-shirt. There is a mound of sand at the foot of the chair, to ease the shock in case he has to jump from his perch to rescue someone. Nearby are a small tank of oxygen and two orange floats. Sixteen-year-old Brito says he hopes he never has to use the oxygen tank or the floats. But the warning whistle that hangs from his neck gets blown frequently. "I use it all the time, like when people go up on those rocks," he says, pointing to an area about seventy-five yards away, jutting out into the water. "They may fall from it. They may get hurt." His stint so far has been relatively uneventful. But he prepares for the worst. "Almost every day when it's hot and sunny, they come out with a dummy, and you've got to do drilling, and show how you could save it. We do running and swimming, about an hour of drills."

To become a lifeguard, Brito took free lessons sponsored by the city. The course was given over a period of three months. "You go to the course for two hours each [session]. There were sixteen of them," for a total of thirty-two hours, he says. "Then you take a test. You've got to know CPR [cardiopulmonary resuscitation] and swim twenty-two laps in the pool, and show you can rescue. They put a [dummy] victim in a pool and you have to pull it out. Then once you pass that, you get to come here."

He arrives at nine forty-five in the morning and works till six-fifteen in the evening, six days a week. "[The job is] pretty good," he says, "but I'm planning to do something different later on [in life], like fixing planes. I want to go into the Air Force someday."

At Coney, Brito is assigned to a group of three lifeguards, the closest one of whom sits approximately a hundred yards away. Asked if he's ever afraid about the prospect of confronting a life-threatening situation, he says, "No, because even if you're rescuing someone, and someone [out of panic] tries to drown you, you're not scared, because you've trained for that."

During their employment, the roughly 900 seasonal lifeguards hired by the city are members of District Council 37. They work between May and the end of August, and during that time they have insurance that covers prescription medications and hospitalization if they are injured on the job.

Brito is about to enter his junior year at Bushwick High School, where he competes in freestyle and butterfly races for the swimming team.

III. THE MONEY AND POWER PROFESSIONALS

30. MARKET TRADER

Salary: $50,000 to $60,000 a year (but expects to earn up to $200,000 the following year)

Hours: 7:30 A.M. to 4:30 P.M., Monday through Friday

Benefits: Health

Union: No

Experience or Requirements: Majored in economics, passed broker's exam

Use computer: Yes, heavily

Workplace/Environment: Desk with computers

Risks: Stress, lots of stress

When he gets to his office at 7:30 A.M., Brook Danaher Bennett doesn't exactly relish the hours that lie ahead. But the money he expects to make is good. And for the time being that's enough of an incentive. At age twenty-four, Bennett is the youngest trader at a small hedge fund. His company lets him buy and sell stocks during the course of the day, and when the day is done he tallies up his profits and losses, sharing the gains with his bosses. Such work is called "proprietary trading." Traders at firms like his typically get between 30 and 50 percent of the profits they make. Too many losses and they're out the door. "The turnover rate can be very high," Bennett says. New traders sometimes "will be gone in two weeks." He plans on staying around long enough to make a bundle, and he starts his morning by devouring the *Wall Street Journal*. "Then I do technical analysis, which is looking at the charts and stuff, the price of the stocks. Basically I do research to collect some ideas for that day. I do that for a good solid two hours, because the market actually opens at nine-thirty." Then the intensity really kicks in. Until four o'clock, virtually without stop, he's researching and making trades.

There are four computer monitors on his desk: one to send orders to the floor of the stock exchange, two that carry financial news, and a fourth that allows him to buy and sell not only on the New York Stock Exchange but on other markets as well. He has two phones. The office can be a madhouse as his fellow traders, several of whom share his long desk, make frenzied decisions. "They're shouting out what they think and what they're hearing from their people and what they're doing. And you've got people swearing and slamming their phones, and you've got these stress explosions every once in a while from different spots." Sometimes, says Bennett, "There're days when I sit at my desk and I want to vomit, you know, and my stomach cramps, and it's just fairly unpleasant." But then again, there are days when it all seems so easy because he buys low and sells high and the money just keeps coming in.

After four o'clock he starts to calculate his profits and losses. So far, because he's just learning, he hasn't been working with tremendous amounts of money. There's a limit of about a million dollars on the amount he's allowed to lose in a day. Once he proves himself, he expects to make around $200,000 a year. His firm is located on Third Avenue, just south of Bennett's East Side apartment. The firm requested that its name not be used. "At this point you could say it's month to month. In any given month I could earn anywhere from nothing to—even though I haven't made it yet, the potential is there, easily—sixty-thousand even in a month. So the variation is extreme." Sometimes, when he has moments to think about it, he feels as if he's playing a numbers game devoid of any real meaning beyond monetary profit. "I feel in one sense that our firm creates nothing, produces nothing," the recent graduate of Vassar College says, "and in that sense, that bothers me sometimes....I'm enough of an intellectual to still feel like something is lacking." If a person is not making well into six figures, he says, "I don't think the stress is worth it."

31. SECURITIES AND ORGANIZED CRIME LAWYER

Salary: Above $500,000 a year

Hours: Often 12 to 17 a day, sometimes 7 days a week

Benefits: Health, Keogh retirement plan, vacation

Union: No

Experience or Requirements: Hofstra Law school, prosecutor's office, securities firm

Use computer: Yes

Workplace: Office in the financial district

Risks: Overwork

Michael Bachner is by his own description a driven man and a control freak. When he's trying a case, he will show up at his office at 5:30 A.M., spend the better part of the day in court, and then return to his office, where he makes calls, writes letters, and continues researching his case until about eleven-thirty at night. His sleep at these times is fitful, because he's thinking about the day before and the day that lies ahead.

Most of his cases involve securities crimes, in which brokers are alleged to have cheated clients by improperly investing their money. Sometimes he represents the bilked clients, other times the brokers. He also does criminal work, and he says he knows that some, if not most, of his clients have committed the crime of which they are accused. Does the knowledge that he might be defending someone guilty of serious fraud or murder bother him? "If a criminal defense lawyer makes moral judgments about the conduct of his client, he's in the wrong business," says Bachner, forty-two, who has a background as a prosecutor of racketeers with the Manhattan District Attorney's office and as an associate vice president with Prudential Securities. "A good criminal lawyer in my opinion is less concerned with what the truth is and more concerned with what the proof is. Truth is not what a jury has to find. The jury has to conclude whether there's proof beyond a reasonable doubt."

Bachner's approach to his job will serve him well in the upcoming weeks, as he prepares to defend John Pappa, an alleged associate in the

Colombo crime family who was accused of killing four people in 1993 and 1994 as part of an underworld turf war.

In some past trials, Bachner has had to go through documents that, when piled up, reached the ceiling. "It can be five hundred to six hundred hours of prep time to review the documents." His clients expect it of him, especially those facing criminal charges. "I know I wouldn't want to spend even three seconds in jail," he says.

Some trials can last as long as six months, and for such cases he generally charges a flat fee in "the high six figures." Hourly rates vary but normally are in the "$300 an hour and up" range. The firm of Bachner & Gehn has more than a hundred active cases. Because every hour of his time is precious, Bachner is happy that he moved his office from his previous location on the East Side of Manhattan, where heavy traffic meant sometimes traveling up to four hours to get back home to New Jersey at the end of the day. He recently rented offices near Wall Street, which is much more accessible to public transportation, and he takes the PATH train under the river, a commute of about an hour. An added benefit is that he is closer to many of his financial district clients.

To relieve tension, Bachner works out at home several times a week, doing aerobics and weightlifting. He takes about two weeks of vacation a year with his family, generally going to the Caribbean or Hawaii. "Sometimes I meet attorneys who have no stress, and I'm amazed," says Bachner, a graduate of Hofstra Law School. He supposes those unstressed lawyers either "don't really care" or are able to delegate much of their responsibilities. Either way is not his nature, he says. "We like what we do, but it is a high-pressure business."

32. APPELLATE JUDGE, STATE OF NEW YORK

Salary: $144,000 a year
Hours: 70, 7 days a week
Benefits: Health, pension, vacation
Union: No

Experience or Requirements: Law school, bar exam, election to bench
Use computer: Yes
Workplace: Office and courtroom
Risks: None reported

Most weekdays Justice William C. Thompson is in his spacious chambers, reading briefs and transcripts and law books in preparation for the two dozen or so cases he and his three colleagues will hear the following Monday. "That's why I can dress like this," he says on a Tuesday afternoon, referring to his velour-type pullover shirt. As a Justice of the Appellate Division of the State Supreme Court, Thompson hears appeals from cases decided in the lower courts. In his job, reading is virtually constant. Often, especially on Saturdays and Sundays, he gets up at five-thirty in the morning and begins going through his files of legal papers. "On Mondays when the attorneys will come in, I will know every single comma and dot that's in their briefs," says Justice Thompson, who is seventy-four and less than two years away from the mandatory retirement age for appellate judges.

Monday mornings, in their Brooklyn courtroom, Justice Thompson and the three other jurists in his "bank" listen to attorneys argue their cases. They ask questions, take notes, make observations. Then they go to lunch, and reassemble in the afternoon to decide on each of the matters. Do the discussions ever get heated? Justice Thompson can remember only once in about twenty years of appellate work that he raised his voice in anger with his colleagues. "We disagree without being disagreeable." If there is a tie vote, the matter can be settled on Wednesdays, when all twenty justices from the Second Department (which covers seven counties in New York State) gather to discuss their cases. A fifth judge is appointed to break a deadlock.

Appellate judges are accorded a deference reserved in other societies for royalty. "An appellate judge," says Justice Thompson, leaning back comfortably, "is defined as one who talks to God, and who gives God only advice." For Justice Thompson, some of the most gut-wrenching cases involve people serving decades in prison for possessing small amounts of narcotics. Justice Thompson believes some of the convicted drug possessors deserve to be free, but New York's harsh "Rockefeller" laws mandate the long sentences. And so he and his colleagues must reject the appeals, he says. "You can claim it's harsh, but the legislature's got to change the law first. We're bound by what the legislature does." The day he was interviewed, the case on Justice Thompson's desk involved an insurance claim resulting from a fire that destroyed a restaurant in Westchester County. A lower court trial determined that there had been arson, and the insurance company was therefore not liable. But the owner was now appealing to Justice Thompson and his colleagues, maintaining he was not responsible for the 1992 fire and that the insurance company owed him $850,000.

In addition to the twenty justices in the Second Department, there are thirty others sitting in other appellate departments covering other parts of the state. They are elected to fourteen-year terms.

A graduate of Brooklyn Law School, Justice Thompson is a Democrat. He has been offered higher-paying positions with law firms, and he may go to one of them when he retires. But for the time being, life is good. He walks to the stately granite appellate division building from his home two blocks away in Brooklyn Heights. Appellate courts are closed during the summer months. "I like what I do...and I don't need a lot of money anymore. I have a house in Brooklyn. I have a house in the country. I have the boat....What the hell else am I looking for?"

33. POLITICALLY CONNECTED LAWYER

Salary: Above $250,000 a year

Hours: 60 a week, 6 days

Benefits: Health, self-provided 401K investment plan, vacation

Union: No

Experience or Requirements: Law school, former member of Congress, former deputy mayor

Use computer: Yes

Workplace: Large East Side office

Risks: Ill-considered public comments

Fischbein, Badillo, Wagner, Harding is the most politically powerful law and lobbying firm in New York City. You're a real estate owner and want a zoning change? Go to them. You've got another problem requiring the attention of a city agency? Go to them. Hundreds of clients choose Fischbein, Badillo simply because it is aggressive and thorough. The estate of Tupac Shakur, the murdered rap star, is being handled by the firm.

But influence is one of the firm's biggest commodities, and the partner with the strongest ties to Republican Mayor Rudolph Giuliani is Herman Badillo, a Puerto Rican–born former congressman who rose to prominence in the 1960s, '70s, and '80s as a progressive Democrat. Now he is an adviser to Giuliani and a Republican. His value to Giuliani is that he frequently argues the administration's line on issues affecting Hispanics and blacks in the city. He is, among other things, chairman of the Board of Trustees of the City University of New York, where he speaks out for what he calls "higher standards" and against remedial programs at the city's public colleges.

About half of Badillo's workweek is spent on such outside activities, which are, in effect, funded by the firm. Recently, for instance, Badillo appeared on the local cable news station, New York 1, defending the mayor's position of wanting to give public money, or "vouchers," to parents sending their children to private schools. Before accepting the invitation to appear on New York 1, "I called City Hall and they said, yes, I should go, and they gave me some basic background information."

Badillo sometimes argues cases in court. "The last time I was in court, last month, was in Queens. That involved a bank foreclosure of a commercial property. We were representing the person who had the mortgage." He also spends dozens of hours a week reading memos and briefs, such as one regarding a firm's client who owns a building in midtown Manhattan and wants to convert it from industrial to residential use. Although ties to the Mayor would seem to help in such cases, Badillo pointedly denies that he is an influence peddler.

In his large eighteenth-floor office on Manhattan's East Side, the walls are lined with memorabilia and photos spanning decades of public service. He is currently a member of the Advisory Committee on the Judiciary under Giuliani. On a typical day, he gets up at about five-thirty in the morning and takes a run of five or six miles through Central Park. (Badillo, age sixty-nine, has finished eleven New York City marathons.) He then heads back to his East Side residence, where he has breakfast and reads the morning papers. After walking to the office, he checks phone messages, looks at his e-mail, and reads the Spanish-language newspapers delivered there every morning. The rest of the day is a mix of legal work, speaking engagements, and "pro bono" activities, such as his frequent meetings with the CUNY Board of Trustees. He is a graduate of City College and Brooklyn Law School. Badillo says that "you've got to be tough" to survive in New York's rough-and-tumble political world. He was tested a few months later, after he made public remarks offensive to Mexicans. Badillo says he apologizes for the comments, but his critics are calling for his dismissal from the CUNY board. He says that being a tough New Yorker, he will survive the controversy.

34. ASSISTANT VICE PRESIDENT AND BRANCH MANAGER OF A BANK

Salary: $57,000 a year
Hours: 40 a week, 5 days a week
Benefits: Health, pension, vacation
Union: No
Experience or Requirements: Teller, other bank experience

Use computer: Yes
Workplace: A neighborhood branch of Fleet Bank
Risks: Being a people person in a computer world

Judith A. Grosch once loved being a bank officer, but that was before banks started buying each other up and replacing tellers with ATMs. Don't get her wrong, she says. Many of the younger managers at Fleet seem to like the job. After all, it involves spending hours at a computer terminal, which many of them seem to enjoy. What's more, the younger ones are coming in making $60,000 a year, even more than Grosch, a twenty-six-year veteran, makes. But Grosch is a people person, and she thinks banks are no longer people places.

In this era of interconnectivity, banks have been encouraging customers to do banking by computer or telephone, and they've been hiring fewer people to work with the walk-ins. As a consequence, customers going to their neighborhood branches often find snaking lines and harried employees. At her branch in Long Island City, Queens, the fifty-four-year-old Grosch supervises three tellers and a customer service person. She's supposed to have an assistant manager, but that position has been unfilled. Up to seventy-five customers enter the branch every weekday, and Grosch and the other employees have to deal with each of them quickly. Ten years ago, a branch like hers would have had nine rather than four people helping the customers, she estimates. Grosch—who is quick with a smile and a "Can I help you?"—spends up to six hours a day at her terminal, opening accounts and "researching into customers' complaints." She works in an open "platform" area that is about the size of a small kitchen.

Grosch is just months away from retiring. She says that, among bank veterans, she is one of the lucky few. Others have been forced to take buyout packages—one-time payments of six months' to a year's pay—or they have been fired outright. Like many veteran managers, Grosch began as a teller and worked her way up the ladder. She does not have a college degree.

The policy of many banks once was to keep employees close to home, but these days managers are transferred every two years or so, Grosch says. Many of the younger, eager-beaver ones don't mind that, but Grosch does. She drives two hours to and from her home in Brooklyn. In her first week at the Long Island City branch, she struggled to find parking in the street, and racked up $200 in parking tickets. Finally, her district manager agreed to reimburse her for the cost of private parking. "Before, they kept you as close as they possibly could to home, and it made sense, because in the old days the object was for someone to go into an office and develop a customer base. And you got to know the family and develop relationships." When Grosch started as a teller, her employer was Bankers Trust, which then became National Westminster, which then became Fleet. The buyouts and firings of her old friends have left her somewhat bitter. Plus, the bank is bringing in more and more young people with college degrees and hard-sell personalities, who are willing to work "ungodly" hours, way beyond the forty she puts in. "Of course we're not the only industry that's doing it, but it doesn't make it any easier," she says.

IV. THE NEW-MEDIA WORKERS

35. WORLD WIDE WEB COORDINATOR

Salary: $50,000 a year
Hours: 8 a day, 5 days a week
Benefits: Health, vacation
Union: No

Experience or Requirements: Know HTML, the coding for the Internet
Use computer: Yes
Workplace: Office
Risks: Overconfidence, attributable to the boom in New Media jobs

For about half her workday, twenty-eight-year-old Nicole Neopolitan taps away at a computer, writing HTML coding, which looks like a meaningless jumble of arrows and letters. It's not what she set out to do in life. She thinks of herself as the creative type, writing and directing movies and plays. But she finds that lots of creative people like her are winding up in the Web design field. She creates the World Wide Web pages on which companies advertise. HTML stands for Hypertext Markup Language, and an HTML programmer has to punch in just the right combination of characters in order to get the colors, font sizes, and paragraph breaks needed on a Web page. Even though the work is tedious, young people who are familiar with HTML are finding they are in demand and that the pay isn't bad. "It's probably one of the best things that's happened to me in terms of money, but I feel kind of like a sellout." She learned the craft of Web writing just a year before she got the job with Waters Design Associates. Through a temp agency, she had taken a position that paid $25 an hour that allowed her to learn HTML code with a woman running a small Web design company from her house.

Neopolitan's eight-hour day at Waters Design is unusual, she says, in an industry that is notorious for demanding much longer shifts from its employees. "It's not the typical New Media company where everyone works 8,000 hours." She lives and works in Manhattan. The part of the job she is most uncomfortable with is supervising three other programmers. Half her time is spent making sure their work is up to par and dealing with administrative details. Neopolitan's colleagues are largely Generation

Xers, but among the managerial types are baby boomers who, she says, try to be loose and cool. Of her supervisor, the company's technical director, she says, "He thinks I'm the young hipster, so he tries to use lingo like 'phat'." Which means cool, by the way.

Neopolitan went to college in Minnesota. Because her HTML skills can get her a job anywhere, her confidence has grown. This sense of security endures even through an anxious time in the New Media industry. Waters Design, for instance, recently lost its main account, IBM. Four workers were let go, and she and others thought Waters might have to lay off more. In her anxiety, Neopolitan went job hunting and quickly learned how valuable she is. "I started to look for other jobs and...I would go on interviews and get offers the next day," she says. "This is when I realized that I was such a sellout."

Neopolitan is halfway through a graduate program in film at Columbia University, and she harbors notions of making it in that industry. Many of her colleagues have the same conflicts. "Most of the people I work with have...outside pursuits," she says. She does worry about becoming frustrated in her job. And she daydreams about selling one of the three movie scripts that she's written. "I keep thinking I should get an agent, maybe I should go to L.A.," she says. "I'm still laboring under the delusion that someone is going to knock on my door and read my script."

36. ASSOCIATE EDITOR WITH AN INTERNET MAGAZINE

Salary: $21,000 to $25,000 a year	**Experience or Requirements:** Wrote articles for community newspaper, did papers on the Web at Brown University
Hours: 10:00 A.M.–7:00 P.M., 5 days a week generally, but often extra work at home	
Benefits: None	**Use computer:** Heavily
Union: No	**Workplace:** Cluttered cubicle
	Risks: Repetitive stress injury

Sitting in her tiny cubicle where a Sony monitor is the center of her attention, Amanda Griscom starts her mornings by surfing the Internet. She looks for interesting news about cultural conflict, foreign affairs, or social policy. Together with her five colleagues, she writes and edits articles that are published on the *Feed* magazine Web site. She also helps determine the layout of the site, what colors and graphics to use, and what audio and video links the site will have.

Griscom, age twenty-three, is an associate editor at *Feed*, an electronic magazine, or "e-zine," which specializes in news commentary and cultural criticism, and which takes its name from the "feeding" process by which words, video, and audio are transmitted across the Internet. The virtual publication has very real ambitions of competing with old-line periodicals such as *Harper's* and *Atlantic Monthly*. Much like others in the New Media industry, which is growing by the nanosecond, the enthusiastic workers at *Feed* are bracing themselves for expansion. "Recently we went from weekly content to daily content," Griscom says.

Feed is a part of Silicon Alley, that enclave in lower Manhattan with concentrations of New Media companies. Though Silicon Alley ventures are rich in potential, they often function on shoestring budgets, as does *Feed*. In spirit, *Feed* hovers somewhere between Wall Street and the city's publishing community. With regard to salaries, "we're more like publishing than Wall Street," says Stefanie Syman, co-founder and co-owner.

Even so, the hackers are not slackers. "There is a twenty-four-hour commitment," Griscom says of herself and her co-workers. Griscom inhabits an insular world in which she and colleagues socialize together and talk continually about the new medium that is changing the world. Her boyfriend Joey Cavella is the publisher of a soft-porn Internet magazine called *Nerve*. They attend endless streams of parties thrown by Internet businesses in lower Manhattan, where they reside. New York City currently has about 23,000 jobs in the New Media market, and the number in a couple of years will be close to 120,000, says Eileen Shulock, program director of the New York New Media Association, a trade group. Large numbers of the industry's employees are like Griscom—Generation Xers with elite educations—who see themselves as explorers of territory that may one day yield abundant wealth for the mind—and, hopefully, for the wallet.

At Brown University, Griscom began to study the universe of hyper-textuality, the World Wide Web's ability to endlessly link words and graphics, so that a person can stop reading midstream and click on pictures, audio, or articles that are related to the original topic. As a senior, Griscom wrote a thesis on hypertext: "Trends of Anarchy and Hierarchy: Comparing the Cultural Repercussions of Print and Digital Media." She blushes now, saying she is much more down-to-earth than the title implies. Griscom likes to think of herself as mostly a journalist or a writer. At other Internet news organizations, especially the television networks or the major newspapers that have Web sites, she would be called a producer.

In a business that is changing so rapidly, is she concerned about what the future holds? "I can't worry about it," she says. "That's one of the things about being in the Web world. Nobody knows what's going to happen in it, where it's going to go. At this point in my life, I just kind of live day to day."

V. THE SKILLED LABORERS

37. LOCKSMITH

Salary: About $26,000 a year
Hours: 8 to 10 a day, 6 days a week
Benefits: Vacation
Union: No

Experience or Requirements: License from city consumer affairs department, which fingerprints and investigates all applicants
Use computer: No
Workplace: A hardware store and people's homes
Risks: Cuts, nicks

Many locksmiths are on call twenty-four hours a day. Albert Lopez began his career that way, but as he got older he decided he wanted to be home with his wife and son in the evenings.

Lopez now works on "a steady basis" out of a hardware store in Woodside, Queens, where he is employed as the full-time locksmith. He makes keys and goes out on as many as ten calls a day, fixing apartment or car locks. "I learned from a friend of mine. He was at another hardware store, and he taught me this business." Lopez, thirty-one years old, is licensed by the city Department of Consumer Affairs. In order to become a locksmith, he says, "Two choices you got. You can go to school for ten months and pay the fee. The second is if you already know the business, you need two official locksmith operators to give you a written letter to say you're fit to be a locksmith. I have friends who are in the locksmith business, and they signed for me." Lopez has had his license for more than ten years, and has worked for several hardware stores. One of his responsibilities is to greet customers as they walk in the front door. He also performs miscellaneous chores for his current boss, a Korean immigrant.

Because he has a skill, Lopez figures he can work at any number of hardware stores around town, if he chooses. "There are over one hundred different types of locks. I deal with cars. I deal with alarms. I deal with safes. That's a real locksmith. I do all that. There's a lot of wannabe locksmiths, and they don't know hardly anything." A large number of his calls are house calls, from people just moving into a new apartment or, less frequently, from someone whose apartment or home has been broken into. "I

go to a house and I give them a free estimate. I recommend what's good for the door. If they like it, they buy it, and I install it for them." Lopez lives in Woodside, just two blocks from his job. "A licensed locksmith averages from $450 to $650 per week—that depends on what kind of locksmith," he explains. "Mine is around $500."

It's better for a locksmith to repair a lock than to sell a new one because a repair job is "all profit," Lopez informs. "I can use my skills instead of using parts. You see, locksmithing is all here," he says, pointing to his head. "If I didn't like my work, I would go into a different career."

38. GARMENT WORKER

Salary: About $25,000 a year, if working steadily and if the bosses pay	**Experience or Requirements:** Sewing ability
Hours: 12 a day, 6 days a week	**Use computer:** No
Benefits: None	**Workplace:** Hot "sweatshops"
Union: Yes	**Risks:** Abusive, nonpaying employers, INS raids

On the twelfth floor of a dank old building on West Thirty-Ninth Street in New York's garment center, two dozen seamstresses sit in rows, their eyes fixed downward on pieces of cloth they are tailoring. Every five seconds, a worker pushes a blouse through a huge clanky "buttoner" device, which makes a whirring noise that reverberates through the shop. Constantly through the twelve-hour day, there is the whine of sewing machines churning out hundreds of blouses for fashion designers and retail outlets around the city.

One of the owners grabs a piece of garment from one of the young seamstresses and then shakes the unfinished blouse, speaking angrily to the blank-faced worker. Silvia Arellano, age forty-nine, is one of the workers at Angela's clothing shop today. Like many of the city's 80,000 garment workers, she is an immigrant, and she has worked for nine years as a seamstress in various shops in the city. Many of her memories are unpleasant. She tells a story about a stint at another sweatshop on West Thirty-Seventh Street. "The *señora* was angry because the girl sewed something wrong and it had to be thrown away. She beat her on the shoulder. It made me so angry I quit two days later."

It was not the first time she got angry and took action. One former boss owed her $3,315 in back pay. Arellano went and complained to the State Department of Labor, which made a ruling in her favor. But sweatshops are notorious for suddenly changing names and locations, and the owner has thwarted attempts to recoup the back pay.

Inside the sweatshops, even with the several big whirling fans, the heat can be very oppressive. The work is constant, and the pressure to produce is intense. "I make maybe 500 to 600 blouses in a day," Arellano says.

And then there are the raids by the U.S. Immigration and Naturalization Service. "There have been raids, and they have taken friends of mine. They raided Mr. Chin (with whom she once worked). He has three factories. They took fifteen people, including four friends of mine. They are being sent back."

A seamstress must know how to use at least one of several different machines that sometimes require a month of instruction to master. "I know how to operate them all," the Mexican-born Arellano says, puffing out her chest and poking an index finger toward it. Sometimes she thinks about how nice it would be to open a garment shop of her own. She would like to have a place where immigrants, especially those here illegally, could work in more humane conditions. "I ask myself what it would take to have my own factory, to help people who don't have *documentos*," says the Bronx resident. "I think about it from time to time. It's just an idea....But who knows?"

39. IRONWORKER

Salary: $49,900 a year
Hours: 40 a week
Benefits: Health, pension, vacation
Union: Yes
Experience or Requirements: Written test, physical test (checking for fear of heights)

Use computer: No
Workplace: A construction site
Risks: Physical injury from falls and other mishaps

George Drossel is part of a crew of ironworkers constructing a new building for Bernard Baruch College, part of the City University of New York. A normal day would find him high up along the frames, walking across the beams. But this Wednesday he is on modified duty. Drossel is still feeling the sting of the twenty-five-foot fall he took the Friday before, when he was knocked down by a beam that was being hoisted to the floor where he was working. The beam got stuck against a piece of metal, and then suddenly "it just spun out of control," Drossel recalls.

"As I saw it, I was trying to get out of harm's way, and in the process of doing that I lost my balance and fell to the beam on the floor below." Then he fell again to the next level, "on my butt," and was taken by ambulance to Bellevue Hospital, where doctors stitched up his right shin. "It could have been fifty times worse," he says. It's pretty obvious why he and his co-workers wear hard hats.

On a normal day Drossel works with scores of other construction workers, catching and putting into place beams that can weigh as much as eight tons. People stop and gawk at the ironworkers walking along the frames of high-rise buildings-in-progress. Drossel likes being up in the air. As part of the physical test to become a member of the union, candidates have to climb up a twelve-foot column, slide across a beam, and climb down another twelve-foot column.

A member of Local 40 of the powerful ironworkers union, Drossel, age twenty-seven, has been doing this work for nine years. He is among the fortunate and well-connected members who have moved seamlessly from one construction job to another over that time. His union is part of his life. The

week before, Drossel showed up at a militant demonstration against a company that was using nonunion labor for a major construction project. But Drossel made it clear he disagreed with the radical unionists who battled with police and wound up all over the evening news. "You had 200 idiots [who] got out of hand," he says.

Even though he gets up at 4:30 A.M. to drive with his buddies from New Jersey to the work site in Manhattan, he looks forward to every working day, Drossel says. He likes being outdoors, he likes the physical work, he likes the camaraderie, the lightheartedness. Drossel has pasted onto his hard hat, among other stickers, a picture of a penis.

He's eager to get back to full duty. "I'm on light detail today, loading trucks. I'll be a go-fer for a couple of days," he says. "It's a nice break for a while. An unfortunate way to get it, but…"

40. WOODWORKER

Salary: $50,000 a year, net
Hours: 10 or 11 a day, weekdays, some weekends
Benefits: None
Union: No

Experience or Requirements: An apprenticeship
Use computer: Yes
Workplace: Two floors of an old building filled with machines and wood
Risks: Nicks from nails and bruises from boards

Andres Mannik's shop is on the edges of the arty and funky Manhattan neighborhood called the East Village. He makes doors, chairs, and assorted other pieces for local businesses. He is a woodworker, he explains, not a carpenter. "A carpenter is generally thought to be someone who works on-site, putting in doors or windows, or frames, or putting in stairs or building a house," he says, "whereas someone like myself would build cabinets or doors."

Most of his income is from small businesses. "I've done for restaurants, I recently did for a bookstore, I've done for video production companies." Working for businesses is easier than dealing with homeowners, he says. Businesses tend to be less finicky; they don't change their mind about the design after the piece is already completed. Mannik's office and shop are located on the basement and first floor of a four-story building he bought in 1988 with several other artisans for $170,000. The owners run the place as a collective. His $650 share of the monthly mortgage is relatively low, considering rents nowadays, he says. In good weather, the sixty-five-year-old Mannik gets to the workshop from his home across town in Chelsea by bicycle. Sometimes he travels on Rollerblades.

The shop is filled with tools, tables, and machines. Nails are an occupational hazard as old as woodworking. But Mannik says injuries have been relatively seldom and minor, never requiring more than a couple of stitches. "I pulled a nail out of my kneecap once," he says matter-of-factly. Mannik does not use a mask to shield his eyes and nose from the dust and chippings that fly when he uses the electric saw. After three decades of doing woodwork, including a stint making huge props for stage productions, he has the confidence of a master when it comes to his tools.

Generally speaking, he does not like to have employees. It's not his nature to be a boss, he says. "I try to avoid having employees because of the paperwork. I have a phobia for bureaucracy." Since the work is on an as-needed basis, he could not keep the employees for long anyway. "I mean, hiring somebody one week, and firing them the next?" he says with a shrug of distaste at the thought. Instead, Mannik sublets his space to other woodworkers, who pay him a percentage of their income from a given job. Mannik reduces his expenses by buying wood and machinery at auctions. On occasion he sells his old machinery there. He has an arrangement with an associate who owns a truck and transports materials and finished work for him.

Mannik spends about a third of his day answering phones, doing paperwork, and making purchases—as opposed to actually building things. He arrives about ten in the morning and stays until eight or nine at night.

Over the years, crime has been a concern in the East Village. Once, in his woodshop, Mannik was robbed at gunpoint. "They just walked in and said they wanted to buy a door. And then pulled a pistol out and said, 'Give me your money.'" He has been burglarized more times than he cares to think about. But Mannik loves the independence of his work, and he believes he has a natural affinity for it. As a child in Estonia, he used to stand and marvel at the men doing woodworking. In the early 1960s, he had a chance encounter at a party with a woodworker who needed an assistant. Soon, he had his own shop. Sometimes during the day, Mannik's mind wanders and he harbors regrets as he thinks of contemporaries who work in government or corporate jobs. "I feel I make a living wage," he says, "but when I look at people, let's say, who got a job somewhere with a company, I would now be on a pension."

41. MECHANIC

Salary: About $26,000 a year
Hours: 60 a week
Benefits: Small contribution from employer toward health
Union: No

Experience or Requirements: Previous work with a garage owner
Use computer: Yes
Workplace: A garage
Risks: None reported

Some car owners like to go to their dealer for servicing. The mechanics are certified by the manufacturer and they periodically attend classes to upgrade their skills. But the exorbitant cost can cause a minor case of apoplexy. And so many owners take their vehicles to a local service station, where they might find a cigarette-smoking veteran mechanic like Joe Alfani.

Alfani, who is forty-two, does basic diagnosis, maintenance, and repairs at the Above All Auto Care Center, located just off the Belt Parkway in the Howard Beach section of Queens. "I learned off the street," says Alfani. "I started getting into cars and motorcycles when I was about sixteen. I just started doing it. Learned off an old-timer who had a station in Coney Island where I grew up." Six days a week, Monday through Saturday, Alfani drives from his home in nearby Broad Channel, arriving at seven-thirty in the morning to begin setting up for the day's work. He starts the compressor, which powers the air tools, and he hauls machines such as the mechanical jack from the garage to outside. Then he and the boss, or the boss's son, decide which cars need to be completed first, and they set up a plan to get through the day.

The work is constant. During the previous week, a school bus company delivered a fleet of its vehicles, two at a time, to be worked on. Alfani had to check out all the systems and the brakes and lights, so they could pass state-mandated inspections. "We must have worked on twenty buses," Alfani says. He has a helper, "the kid," who hits the brakes, for example, while Alfani checks the lights. A rotating group of other employees, immigrants with limited English for the most part, pump gas at the Getty tanks several yards to the left of the garage. Most of the guys take a forty-five-minute lunch break, but Alfani says he generally spends no more than fifteen minutes on his.

Diagnosing and fixing electrical problems can be especially difficult. Electrical problems involve examining complex sets of wires with an array of different colors, which vary according to the make of the car. The station has $150,000 worth of computers, some of them containing specifications and directions for the repair of various car models. The owners, Tony Dell'Era and his son Anthony, generally handle the most complex equipment. Alfani often uses the "snap-on scanner," which connects to a car's computer, so he can determine if the problem is a bad sensor, a faulty switch, or an emissions failure of some kind.

Alfani dropped out of high school in the eleventh grade. But if he didn't love geometry, he loves mechanics. On his off days, Alfani uses his technical abilities on his boat, a nineteen-footer on which he fishes off Sheepshead Bay, Broad Channel, or Coney Island. Although his work is nonstop, he likes it, Alfani says, as he puffs on a Marlboro. He smokes two packs a day. "If you're diagnosing a car, then another person's calling you to look over here, you try not to get wound up....You have a cigarette. Then you walk over to another car....A person comes in with a car, you take the phone number and address. The cigarette just helps me get through the day. At night after supper, I don't smoke at all."

42. CHIEF STAGEHAND

Salary: $75,000 a year

Hours: 40 a week generally, but sometimes twice that

Benefits: Health, pension, vacation pay of about $60 a week, paid to union and disbursed annually to employee

Union: Yes

Experience or Requirements: Stage production work in secondary school and college

Use computer: Yes

Workplace: Theater

Risks: Stretches of time without work

David M. Cohen loves being around music and actors, and as a stagehand he gets to do that a lot. But he also spends much of his time worrying. As head production carpenter, or chief stagehand, it's his job to supervise the crew of carpenters who put together stage props. He has to make sure the mechanical parts move onstage at the right time and that they don't fall on anyone. Most recently, he's been with the musical *On the Town*, which opened in the fall of 1998 at the Gershwin Theatre.

Typically, he works a standard forty-hour week. But when the crew is making props, the schedule can be brutal. Over a ten-week period in the fall of 1998, during preparations for the opening of *On the Town*, Cohen put in eighty- to ninety-hour weeks. Among his responsibilities was the construction of a steel bridge over the stage. His schedule gets more regular after the show opens. But his nerves remain on edge. "I am watching everything that moves. I have a walkie-talkie to communicate with my assistants and a headset to communicate with the stage managers....I watch all moving parts and units, and make sure that moving units are clear of the actors." Because *On the Town* deploys two prop dinosaurs that traveled from the wings to the stage, one of Cohen's main tasks is to "check to make sure that no one is going to get hit by a moving dinosaur."

The activity is continual and intense, but the thirty-five-year-old Cohen gets to enjoy parts of the performances nevertheless. "The [Leonard] Bernstein score is so good that it makes a great backdrop for my day's work," he says. "I can't concentrate on the musical's story because I am too busy working, but at least I can enjoy the music."

Besides endangering someone, a prop that does not move as planned can be embarrassing. During a recent matinee, a hydraulic lift was supposed to bring a prop taxicab up to the deck, but it failed. Panic City. But the actors came to the rescue. Instead of singing in the taxi, as scripted, two of the leads did their duet on chairs that were placed onstage. After that show was over, the carpenters labored through their dinner break and fixed the hydraulic system, which worked for the night performance without a hitch.

He recalls another incident: "A few nights ago, a wagon got stuck on stage into the next scene. I had to run onstage and pull it off. Another stage-hand was right behind me, helping me pull it off before I could even ask for help." Curiously enough, the mishaps loosen the knots in Cohen's stomach. "It is a relief when the worst-case scenario finally happens and it turns out that it can be dealt with quickly and the show is not ruined," he says.

Though plays almost inevitably close after a short time, there is "always the knowledge that there is another show around the corner," and Cohen's periods of unemployment between shows are almost always brief.

43. BROADCAST ENGINEER

Salary: $60,000 to $100,000, depending on overtime	**Experience or Requirements:** On the job
Hours: Sometimes 16 a day	**Use computer:** Yes
Benefits: Health, pension, vacation	**Workplace:** Sometimes a truck, other times an office
Union: Yes	**Risks:** Tripping in cramped confines

Karen Steckler spends half her time working in a truck as part of a crew covering sporting events for ABC. Her job is to operate the "chyron" machine that takes words and numbers and puts them onto the television screen, so that viewers can see football scores, golf statistics, or the names of guests being interviewed. Being with a national network, she often has to travel across the country. She gets to attend exciting meets and matches, but the hours can be brutal. "I've covered six Olympics," she says. On some days, "we work anywhere from a twelve- to sixteen-hour day."

Television people "work to the second," meaning that if they are late showing up, even by mere moments, the whole production schedule is threatened. And the continual rush-rush to arrive on time leads to a lot of stress. "You can't tell *Good Morning America* that they're going on the air at seventeen after the hour because you couldn't park your car. I mean, everything is timed out to the second, so it's a very, very intense position to be in."

She works about half the year in the field and the other half at ABC headquarters in Manhattan. Sometimes she does yearn for a more "normal" life, one in which she doesn't have to work until three in the morning and be far away from home on Thanksgiving or New Year's. Fortunately Steckler, who is fifty years old and commutes to the offices of ABC/Disney from Connecticut, doesn't have children.

On a typical day covering a sporting event out of town, she'll show up at the office (that is, the truck) at about seven in the morning. She'll work with the production assistants and go over the statistics and other information to be put on the television screen. Then she'll proofread copy. This routine is repeated throughout the day, and it can go on for many consecutive days, depending on the event being covered. There are certain hazards to being in a truck all day. About ten years ago, she says, she tripped over some cables and now has a chronic back problem. "Once you've hurt your back, you always have a back problem." She and others are also concerned about the long-term effects of the microwave equipment on the trucks. Besides that, the trucks are often uncomfortable, noisy, and cold, she says. The vehicles must be kept at about sixty-eight degrees because of the electronic equipment, and "the noise level is extremely high, lots of screaming and yelling by irate producers and directors." Adding to the overall discomfort, "we sit for hours in chairs that are not particularly ergonomically correct."

Steckler got her job because "in 1975, EEOC (the U.S. Equal Employment Opportunity Commission) came along and said you must have X amount of females, so train people, pick the best, and give them some of the jobs." Previously she had been secretary to a general manager of engineering at ABC. Because of differences between her union and Disney, the owner of ABC, concerning medical benefits, Steckler and her co-workers were locked out by their employer in 1998, but the dispute was resolved in 1999.

Despite the headaches connected with the job, there is great camaraderie among the employees and, all in all, she says, it can be a lot of fun. "There's a lot of personal gratification about doing a terrific job, seeing a final product on the air, and knowing that you've been part of something that's successful. That's truly a best moment." And, oh yes, she says: "Winning Emmys is very nice. That's a best moment."

44. GRAVE DIGGER

Salary: $35,000 to $40,000 a year   **Experience or Requirements:** Physical strength

Hours: 8 a day   **Use computer:** No

Benefits: Health, pension, vacation   **Work environment:** Cemeteries

Union: Yes   **Risks:** Tripping, cutting hands or feet

Walter Plonski is preparing the grave of someone who will be buried the following day. The dead person will be the third member of the Dean family to go into this plot. The previous family members died in 1978 and 1975. But these particulars mean nothing to Plonski. He has been working as a grave digger at Cypress Hills cemetery for twenty-eight years. And by his own description, he does not have a heart that goes soft at the singing of burial chants, or even, anymore, at the wailing of grieving widows. At funerals, before the praying is done, Plonski and his colleagues stand respectfully off to the side. Then, when the ceremony is over and the casket has been lowered into the ground, they put dirt back in the grave and pat it down. "We're tough here," he says. "Anything they bring, we bury." But then, as if pricked by a sudden recollection, he admits that he does in fact get choked up at times, like at the interment of babies. "You think they might be your own," he says, with a softness that belies his practiced flippancy.

As part of the team that digs graves, Plonski operates a backhoe. Sitting in the cabin of the machine and maneuvering its levers, he piles the dirt onto a "pug," a tiny dump truck. The operator of the pug then drives away to empty the load, weaving in and out of the rows of tombstones. Soon the driver returns so that he and Plonski can continue the process, until the grave is dug. Normally, Plonski doesn't chat much with anyone, especially when he's in the backhoe with the engine running. Except for late at night, when beer-swigging teens or voodoo practitioners might enter, cemeteries radiate the sweet silence of a botanical garden.

There are, to be sure, certain dangers associated with grave digging. The day Plonski was interviewed, another worker "stepped crooked" into a plot and twisted his ankle, seriously injuring it. And then there are the normal risks that go with moving heavy objects, such as tombstones that can weigh more than 200 pounds, or with using grounds-keeping tools. "I lost a piece of a toe with a grass-cutting machine, in about 1971," says union rep James Confessore, who works at the cemetery and was listening in on the conversation with Plonski.

The forty-three-year-old Plonski started out at Cypress Hills in 1969 as a grass cutter when he was fourteen years old. "I never finished high school," he says. "That's why I ended up here, digging graves." Despite the lingering sense of being an underachiever, Plonski, who drives in from his home in Smithtown, on Long Island, likes his work well enough. And he likes the union that stands behind him. Several times over the past thirty years, the grave diggers union flexed its muscles by shutting down cemeteries in New York. "We had over 500 bodies stacked up," Confessore says, speaking with a measure of pride as he recalled a strike in the early 1970s. The grave diggers are represented by Local 74 of the Service Employees International Union.

Plonski compares his job to that of a mailman who works in any kind of weather. "We're here in snow, ice, rain." Then his mind reels back to the winter days when he and his co-workers strain to dig up earth that is rock hard from the bitter cold. "No. This is rougher than being a mailman," he amends.

45. STEAMFITTER/ INSTRUCTOR

Salary: Over $70,000 a year
Hours: 8:00 P.M. to 4:00 P.M., 3 days,
8:00 A.M. to 8:00 P.M., 2 days
Benefits: Health, pension, vacation
Union: Yes

Experience or Requirements: High school diploma, a test, and an apprenticeship
Use computer: Yes
Workplace: Union building, construction site
Risks: Burns, falls

As far as Charles Bellach is concerned, a career in the building trades, especially as a steamfitter, can be every bit as challenging as one that requires a college degree. And it can be as financially rewarding, too. "If you go to college, you have to lay out $50,000 to $60,000, easily," says Bellach, referring to total tuition costs. "You're not making any income, and at the end you may come out with a job that pays $30,000. Here you have an opportunity, assuming we have an industry that's booming, to be an apprentice who's making 40 percent of a journeyman's wages. You're learning and you're working on the job." A journeyman, or full-fledged steamfitter who has gone through his five-year apprenticeship, earns about $55 an hour, which includes benefits.

Steamfitters do a range of jobs associated with construction, including the creation and assemblage of pipes for heating, ventilation, sprinklers, refrigeration, and air conditioning systems. The job involves a technical knowledge of those areas as well as skill in welding. Bellach, who is forty-seven and has more than two decades of experience, teaches welding at the Steamfitters Industry Training Center, run by the steamfitters union and located in an industrial section of Long Island City, Queens. Bellach travels there by public transportation from his home in suburban Westchester County.

A journeyman steamfitter works seven-hour days, five days a week. The downside of the business is that when there's a bad slump in the local economy, such as in the mid-1970s, unemployment in the building trades can run as high as 50 percent. On the average, steamfitters work about ten months out of the year. Bellach himself earns more than $70,000 a year—about $20,000 more than the typical veteran steamfitter—because, as an employee at the union's apprenticeship program, he works a full twelve months of the year. He is effusive and chatty, and says he loves getting his hands dirty with torches and pipes. His desk and file cabinet are filled with books about techniques of steamfitting.

There are 201 apprentices at various levels of the five-year apprenticeship program. By contract, their employers pay them to attend a day of classes once every two weeks. While on their job sites, they work along with a journeyman in a two-person team called a "gang." They also serve as "gofers," fetching coffee, donuts, and lunch for the senior workers. Admission to the apprenticeship is based on interviews with a team of union and industry representatives as well as a test administered by the New York State Department of Labor. Apprenticeships open up only every four years or so. Of 5,000 applications handed out, only about 250 applicants are accepted.

The state stepped into the picture thirty years ago after many people complained that the industry was discriminating against minorities. The union remains largely white although union officials maintain that this is changing. Out of the 201 apprentices currently in the program, 37 are black, 28 are Hispanic, 5 are "others," including Asians, and 18 are women.

The work can be dangerous. For instance, the use of acetylene torches for welding can lead to fires or explosions, and falls on the job are common. And then there is the instability of the work, moving from site to site, job to job, as buildings go up and are completed. "If you can't tolerate some periods of unemployment, if you're someone who requires security above all, then this isn't for you," says Bellach.

46. RODMAN ON SURVEYING TEAM

Salary: About $29,000 a year

Hours: 8 a day, 5 days a week, plus lots of overtime

Benefits: Health, profit-sharing plan, vacation

Union: No

Experience or Requirements: Bachelor's degree in architectural design in his native Belarus

Use computer: No

Workplace: Sidewalks, streets, yards

Risks: Boredom

Sergey Kopytko holds the "rod" or "pole" while a surveyor standing some yards away looks into an electronic measuring device and records the coordinates. He is part of a team that includes two others: the "party chief" Abdool Rahoof and the "transit man" Howard Roberts. Rahoof and Roberts are the surveyors who take turns entering data into the surveying equipment. Kopytko is the youngest of the bunch, just shy of thirty. He is also the low man in status and salary. He moves along the sidewalk or streets, backward or forward at the command of Rahoof or Roberts. He often passes the greater part of the day not saying much of anything at all. In large part, that is because he does not speak English well; only recently did he emigrate from Belarus in the former Soviet Union. Kopytko says he wants to advance in the surveying craft and eventually become an architect. He is taking English at night, four evenings a week, at Long Island University in Brooklyn, where he lives.

The surveying team goes out to an assignment every day from Montrose Surveying in Queens. They have with them about $50,000 worth of equipment, including the computers into which they put the coordinates of sewer, gas, and water pipelines that they survey. Montrose's clients generally are architects or engineers who want to know where to place new lines. On this particular day, the trio is working at a small shopping complex off Cross Bay Boulevard. The mall's owner wanted to make improvements to his lines serving stores such as Dairy Mill, Sleepy's, and Lady Jane Craft Center. The team walks around taking measurements, with Rahoof and Roberts using the computer equipment and barking orders to Kopytko: "Move back! ...Move to the right!"

Normally, a rodman like Kopytko is eventually promoted to transit man and then to crew chief, and his pay increases accordingly. By far the greatest number of those entering the surveying field are recent immigrants, many of whom, like Rahoof and Roberts (both from Guyana in South America), have had experience in their native countries.

If Kopytko were able to get a rodman's job with a union shop, he would probably earn about twice what he's getting at Montrose. He gets $10 an hour when the job is contracted with a private company. But he gets twice that—union scale—when the contract is with a government agency. Over the course of a year, Kopytko's average pay is about $14 an hour. The attraction of Montrose Surveying is that the work is steady. All the workers at Montrose earn overtime, up to twenty additional hours a week beyond their normal forty, getting paid time and a half for it. Rahoof says, "A job is very easy to get in this profession. A lot of people don't want to do it when it gets cold. Out there it's tough when it gets cold. I don't think people want to work out there." Kopytko grew accustomed to cold in his homeland. What he longs for now is the day when he will be able to call himself a survey technician and bark commands in English.

VI. THE SERVICE PROVIDERS

47. EXTERMINATOR

Salary: About $31,720 a year	**Experience or Requirements:** On the job
Hours: 40 a week	**Use computer:** No
Benefits: Health, pension, vacation	**Workplace:** Basements, kitchens, yards
Union: Yes	**Risks:** Bites and fumes

William Diaz loves it when his clients look relieved and thankful to see him. At these moments, he is their conquering hero, the man who rescues them. The villains are mostly rats and roaches. Diaz, thirty-three years old, is a "service technician" with Acme Exterminating. For his company's clients throughout Manhattan, he inspects cracks and crevices, lays down traps, and uses chemicals to kill insects and rodents. Occasionally, he's chanced upon frightened rats that leaped on him. Once, he was putting his hand into a garbage can, inspecting bait he had laid down, when a rat jumped on his arm. He tried to shake it off. "I was in mortal combat," says Diaz, who used to wrestle professionally years ago under the nickname Swan. He was bitten, and finally had to kill the rat "the old-fashioned way. I took a stick and put it to its throat." Reflecting on that occasion, he recalls, "I wanted to quit right then and there."

Diaz's days are generally more routine than that. He carries sixteen pounds of materials and equipment in his knapsack, and travels around town by public transportation, which he also uses to get to work from his home in Brooklyn. One day finds him at a day-care center in East Harlem, one of Acme's clients. Diaz goes through the kitchen and inspects previously laid insect strips to see if there are any bugs on them. (There are seven flies.) He put down other strips. Into areas around the sink and stove he releases a "fogger," which creates a mist and draws insects out. He also has at his disposal quick killers such as PT 270, and "residual" pesticides, like Dursban, which works for weeks but does not have quite the same zapping effect as PT 270. The strongest killer in his arsenal is BP 300, which he uses only as a last resort. "It always gives me a headache," he says. "It's a very rare thing that it's used ... but it's a fantastic tool." Despite having so many chemicals, Diaz says his company is into IPM, which stands for Integrated Pest Management. He encourages his clients to keep a clean environment and to use baits and traps rather than potentially dangerous chemicals. He particularly avoids strong pest killers at the day-care center. Selling people on IPM isn't always easy, especially for folks accustomed to the old-time exterminators whose work consisted almost entirely of walking around the premises with their little tanks and spraying into corners. "Some people, they don't see the tank, they don't want the service," he says. There are times when the ebullient Diaz becomes a bit dejected on the job. On occasion, he's heard insensitive clients refer to him as "rat boy" or "bug man." "It bothers me," he says.

Diaz knows his business. Listening to him talk about rats, for instance, is like reading from a pest encyclopedia. "Rats don't have good vision, and so they feel safer having their whiskers pass near the base of a wall," he says. "Rats are also neophobic, which is the fear of something new. If you place bait stations down, a rat senses a change in environment. I've seen places where that [a bait station] was enough to scare off the rats.... The rat sensed a rat." Diaz can also explain the chemical bases and effects of chemicals he uses. He's personable and well spoken, and the clients like him. A high school dropout who later went back to earn an equivalency diploma, he is a member of Local 32B–32J of the Service Employees International Union.

Diaz likes to believe he's helping people and helping the environment. He also helps himself by wearing plastic gloves, when necessary, and by trying to be careful. One or two bad experiences have taught him to remain cautious: "You always have to be careful, because when you put bait in a hole, you never know if there's gonna be a rat popping out."

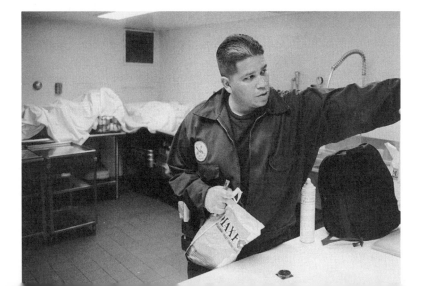

48. BARTENDER

Salary: $45,032 a year, including tips   **Experience or Requirements:** On the job
Hours: 40 a week   **Workplace:** Bar
Benefits: None   **Risks:** Drunk patrons, broken liquor
Union: No   glasses, and cigarette smoke

Gerad Argeros reaches the L-Ray Bar in Greenwich Village, where they serve up Tex-Mex style food and drink, at about four o'clock in the afternoon. He has a cup of coffee and chats, then begins the tedious process of hauling up the ice, booze, napkins, and everything else he'll need for a night of bartending.

People go to bars to relax and unwind, and Gerry enjoys shooting the breeze with honest, easygoing folks. So, by and large the evenings go well. But there are minuses on the tab. Often the shifts are excruciatingly routine. Get the order, fix the *mojito,* serve the customer, take the cash, move on to the next customer. And standing up for eight to ten hours an evening can be rough on the spine. At the age of twenty-eight, he suffers from back pain.

But possibly worse than all that are the hassles of dealing with tanked-up customers, some of whom are downright insulting. "You take it home with yourself in the sense that, 'Man, what am I doing with my life that I'm sitting here being berated by people?' You know, some guy calls me a fucking faggot or a fucking. S.O.B., or a million other things. Like I've been called everything, you know?"

He also has to deal with the moral issue of serving alcohol to people who appear unable to do things like drive home safely, much less carry on a civil conversation. "At some point I've got to say, 'No, you don't get any-more.'" The conflict—between selling drinks so his boss can make money and, on the other hand, making sure that no one gets hurt—weighs on him. "I'm kind of like a gatekeeper in that sense, to ensure that, like, the guy doesn't hurt somebody," he says. "If someone's mentally ill, do you serve them? I've seen lives that are being slowly eaten away by alcohol. There are people who would come in and sit at the bar that I was working at every single day, some starting at eleven-thirty in the morning...but

they're spending money. It's a bummer, part of what you're doing; it's a business, and it depends on that money....I just don't know that I'm the one to judge all the time when somebody needs to stop drinking. You know, I don't know. I don't know that I'm trained...you know."

Sometimes, even as he smiles and starts to mix whiskey sours or get a beer, he wonders whether a guy as smart as he should be going to college and doing something else. But he goes on. "I do last call at twelve-thirty in the morning," he says. "You close up, you clean everything up...count your money, count the bills, rectify the money that you owe the house, take your tips, usually have a beer." He and other bartenders get together often after work and talk over their problems. He generally walks to his apartment in the East Village, a fifteen- or twenty-minute trek. Sometimes he finds it hard to go right to sleep after a night's work tending bar.

49. NEWSSTAND CLERK

Salary: Less than $13,000 a year	**Experience or Requirements:**
Hours: 8 a day, 6 days a week	On-the-job training
Benefits: None	**Use computer:** No
Union: No	**Workplace:** A five-foot by three-foot enclosure
	Risks: Confrontations with thieves

Kamal Muhammad can stand, sit, and move his arms, but not much else. He sells newspapers, magazines, candy, and cigarettes in the confining space of a roofed sheet-metal newsstand, at the bustling northwest corner of Eighty-Second Street and Broadway in Manhattan.

Most of the time, he doesn't have to say anything. People just reach out, take what they want, and pay him. The newspapers are in the front of the newsstand and the magazines are to the left and to the right. Candy and other junk food is lined up above the newspapers, just within Muhammad's reach. If someone asks for a newspaper, he points to it. If it's a magazine and it's closer to him than to the customer, he'll get it himself. Same thing with candies. Cigarettes are a different matter. The cigarettes are within his reach only, and the customers have to ask him for the brand they want. He gets it, they pay.

Muhammad says his main problem is that some youngsters like to help themselves, free of charge, to a fistful of anything within easy reach. This is the potentially dangerous part of this work. Being short on inventory or cash is not good for job tenure. When the boss comes around he doesn't want to hear about missing money or cigarettes. Besides, Muhammad has his sense of right and wrong, and despite his very evident frailness, he doesn't like to be pushed around. So he spends a portion of his days yelling at youngsters and young adults who pilfer items from him. Sometimes he leaves his booth and runs to chase them. Limited in his English and in any sense of American political correctness, he admits to bearing a well of anger against some young blacks. "Black people is a problem," he tells his interviewer, an African American. "I chase. It's dangerous." The thirty-two-year-old immigrant from India works on the West Side of Manhattan where his customers are generally white and fashionably dressed.

A woman buys a paper, plops down her money, and starts to walk off. But Muhammad calls her back, handing her a wad of nine one-dollar bills. "But honest, I thought I gave you a one," she says. He smiles and moved his head from side to side. She hesitates and then takes the money and moves on. "Do you have any peanut bars?" a young man comes up and asks. Without a word, Muhammad points to the Planters peanut bars sloping away in front of him.

When he has to go to the bathroom, Muhammad closes down for several minutes and has a friend from a nearby store keep his eye on the newsstand. He generally uses the restroom at Barnes & Noble. Living in an inexpensive two-room apartment in Manhattan that he shares with two other immigrants, Muhammad says he would like to return to India someday, to settle and build a house. But earning the money he does now, that may take quite some time, he says.

50. BARBER

Salary: About $11,000 a year	**Experience or Requirements:** Apprenticeship under another barber, barber's license from state health department
Hours: 10 to 12 a day, 6 days a week	
Benefits: None	**Use computer:** No
Union: No	**Workplace:** A small shop
	Risks: Boredom during long waits between customers

Sometimes guys ask him to shave nicknames on their heads, or dye their hair red or green. Juan Hernandez always gives the same reply. "I tell them we don't do that. We send them to the 'salon' down the way," the twenty-two-year-old barber says. His co-worker Julio Carreras chimes in: "We're just regular barbers."

As a regular barber, Hernandez is busiest on Fridays and Saturdays. On a typical Saturday he might have fifteen or more customers, who sit in his chair for about twenty minutes each while he snips and combs. They pay up to $10 per cut, sometimes less. Most of them tip a dollar. Although he earns $350 or so a week, he turns 40 percent of it over to the owner of the shop.

Hernandez is a native of the Dominican Republic, a country where hair textures range from Indian-straight to African-curly, and the young haircutter believes the diversity has benefited him. "We cut all kinds of hair, white people, black people, Hispanic people," he says. Hernandez considers the fifty-seven-year-old Carreras to be his mentor as well as *compañero*. The older man has been cutting hair for forty-three years, much of that time in the Dominican Republic, and is the sponsor on Hernandez's apprentice certificate (issued by the Secretary of State at a cost of $10); but while Hernandez admires his mentor and calls him "El Profesor," he does not want to be practicing the craft quite that long. So he spends idle moments at the Bronx barber shop dreaming about days filled with more excitement. "I would like to be a police officer. Someday I will take the test."

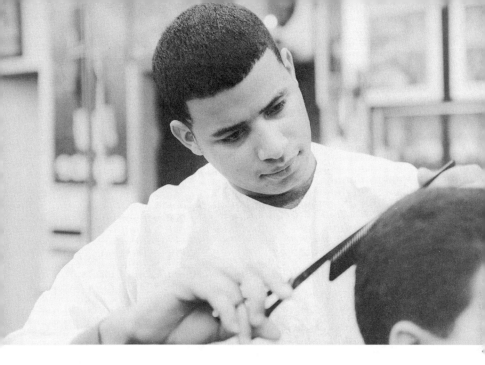

A high school dropout, Hernandez would have to obtain a general equivalency diploma and then attend two years of college and pass a civil service exam before becoming a New York City police officer.

Half an hour earlier, cops in plain clothes had swooped down on a group of alleged drug dealers about twenty yards from the barber shop and arrested them. Hernandez—who lives nearby and drives to work every day—would like a full-time job like that. Recently he had some excitement right *in* the shop, when a customer jumped out of the chair, fighting mad about the haircut Hernandez had given him. The man began cursing, loudly, abusively, menacingly. "I felt bad. He was a handsome guy," Hernandez says remorsefully. "I didn't charge him."

51. BOOKSTORE MANAGER

Salary: $26,000 to $36,000 a year, depending on profits
Hours: 70 a week
Benefits: None
Union: No

Experience or Requirements: A lifetime of loving books
Use computer: Yes
Workplace: Small store
Risks: None reported

"It's not every day someone approaches you with, 'Hey, would you like to do something you love?'" That's the way Marshall Mintz feels about the day a couple of years back when the owners of Partners & Crime Mystery Booksellers came to him with an irresistible offer.

The owners told Mintz that the previous manager of the Greenwich Village bookstore was exhausted from the long hours and wanted out. "After four years in the business, twelve hours a day, six days a week, he was nonstop, and he just wanted to take a break, and they asked me if I wanted the job," Mintz, twenty-nine, recalls. Now Mintz himself is putting in long hours, cleaning the floors, tending to customers, taking orders, introducing guest speakers, and everything else associated with the all-consuming job of managing a small specialty bookstore. Because he has to keep up with new releases, and because he simply enjoys it, he reads up to five hours a day.

At the time the owners came to him about working at the mystery bookstore, he was an assistant stage manager for the musical *Stomp*. Prior to that, just after finishing Colby College, he did a stint as a hand on a logging freighter. But always, always, he read lots of mystery books. Now surrounded by 5,000 paperback and hardcover mystery titles, Mintz feels like a mouse in a fifteen-by-thirty-foot cheese factory.

In addition to the sometimes tedious chores around the bookstore, Mintz hosts a mock radio show there on Saturdays. "We do 'The Shadow,'" he says, offering an example. He gets paid a base salary of about $26,000 a year, but Mintz says the owners have agreed to consider giving him a percentage of the store's profits, which could add another $10,000 to his income. Last year, Partners & Crime grossed $500,000, but he doesn't know how much of that was profit, he says. Mintz owns a co-op apartment just a ten-minute walk from the bookstore.

"Maybe I suck," he says, explaining his willingness to work for a base salary that other college graduates might consider low. Mintz pays for his own health insurance.

He says that small specialty bookstores (unlike small general-interest bookstores) are surviving the onslaught of big chains such as Barnes & Noble. Those huge outlet stores have been luring customers with discounts and coffee shops. Mintz laughs as he mentions reading that one of the big outlets was about to start serving alcohol. What Partners & Crime can offer is unmatched expertise, he maintains. "If a customer says, 'I want a novel about trains that takes place in Africa,' I can refer you to two or three," he says. "We know our material."

52. CIRCUS WORKER

Salary: $50,000 a year
Hours: Often 8:00 A.M. to midnight, 7 days a week
Benefits: Health, vacation
Union: No

Experience or Requirements: Previous circus experience, theater major in college
Use computer: Yes
Workplace: Trailer, tents, office, the road
Risks: None reported

Cheryl Jones still carries her clown costume in her suitcase. But she's more likely to be meeting with architects or talking about workers' compensation than performing for a crowd. Jones, age forty-eight, is the assistant manager of the Big Apple Circus, which plays at Lincoln Center for twelve weeks, beginning in November. She's responsible for dealing with customers, hiring ushers, making sure there's enough electricity, and handling a tent full of other duties.

That's a far cry from how she started out in the business, as a clown with a California circus back in 1975. Jones used to believe that all she wanted to do was be the center of attention, wear costumes, and make people laugh. But now that she's approaching fifty, she feels maybe her clowning days have come and gone. And she's made her peace. These days she delights in the pencil pushing and public relations responsibilities of circus work. After all, she's still in the circus business that she loves. "I thought when I came here, being in management, that I would be able to become a clown again," Jones says of her start with the Big Apple Circus in 1986. "But it's never come to fruition. Which is fine....Now that I'm older, I'm probably physically not real adept to run around and do all that stuff." She adds, "I wear many hats, and that's okay. I'm a workaholic....I like to be in the office and out with the audience."

At Lincoln Center, the troupe always plays to full houses, Jones says. Ticket prices range from $12 to $58. "We get a lot of celebrities that come all the time. It's nice family entertainment." But soon the show will have to hit the road. "We play here until the middle of January," she says, referring to Manhattan, "and then after we tear down here, we go down to

South Carolina for about three or four weeks and we refurbish equipment and catch up on stuff....That's just like a temporary winter quarters.... And then we open in Atlanta and we play the East Coast, and New England, and as far west as Chicago. We go to Atlanta, New Jersey, then Boston for six weeks, and then back to Queens and Long Island." At the end of the summer the circus packs its trailers and returns to its creative center and home base, at Walden, New York, north of New York City. There the circus takes some time off and begins working on the new show, which eventually will take them back to New York City.

53. TELEPHONE COMPANY EMPLOYEE

Salary: About $40,000 a year	**Experience or Requirements:** A written test
Hours: 35 a week	**Use computer:** Yes
Benefits: Health, pension, vacation	**Workplace:** Office
Union: Yes	**Risks:** Repetitive stress injuries for operators

Denise Durant has been working sixteen years for Bell Atlantic, the local phone company that spun off from AT&T. She is an administrative assistant now, and she describes the work as easy. Filing and photocopying mostly. But for thirteen years she was a telephone operator. "Nobody should be an operator after ten years, because you get burnt out on that job," the thirty-nine-year-old Durant says. "Operating is very strict. You get thirty minutes lunch. Two fifteen-minute breaks. You have to raise your hand to go to the bathroom. They sign your name on a board and when they come to you, it's your turn and you can't be gone more than five minutes."

The average Bell Atlantic operator takes about 2,000 calls a day, and their employer rates their performance in part on what's called AWT, or "average work time." When the average working time is 21.5 seconds, an operator is expected to spend no more than that amount of time talking with a caller, Durant says.

Typically about 80 to 100 operators are in an area together. Sitting in little quadrants with partitions, they wear headsets and spend most of their time typing the names of people and businesses into a computer. "The average operator sits at the board two-and-a-half hours before you get a break. They let you bring water [to the workstation] but no eating." Some operators complain of repetitive stress injury, caused by the continual punching of names into the computers.

By Durant's estimate, the ratio of women to men is about eight to one. As an operator, Durant particularly disliked the night shift, even though there is some extra pay for it. Night operators wind up overburdened because there are fewer operators with whom to share the load, she says. Furthermore, they worry about returning safely home on public transportation. "Those who lived in Brooklyn, we would 'buddy up' and all ride together on the train." And last, but not least, they have the problem of finding babysitters to care for their children at night.

Being an active member of her union, the Communication Workers of America, Durant is angered by Bell Atlantic's efforts to downsize its staff. She says the company has been recruiting nonunion people to work outside New York State and paying them $5 to $7 per hour, about a third of what operators in New York City get. She says she hopes to leave Bell Atlantic within several years and start her own business, perhaps a child care center. "I want to open an overnight day-care. I remember working nights and never being able to find day-care. I want to service corrections officers, postal workers, nurses, conductors, transit workers," she says. "It's a moneymaker, too. I'm going to make a lot of money because I'll be the only one doing it at night."

54. SECURITY GUARD

Salary: About $15,500 a year
Hours: 40 a week
Benefits: Vacation
Union: No

Experience or Requirements: Character reference
Use computer: No
Workplace: A homeless shelter
Risks: Being near drugs and other illegal activity

James Johnson works the 8:00 A.M. to 4:00 P.M. shift at the Brooklyn Atlantic Men's Shelter. He spends part of the day patrolling the perimeters of the facility, a converted armory that takes up the better part of a city block and is the temporary residence of 200 homeless men, many of whom have drug problems. Johnson's job is to make sure that only registered residents are allowed into the building and that house rules against sex, drugs, and fighting are obeyed. He is part of a force of twenty-four security guards who earn just above minimum wage.

As far as he is concerned, his low salary does not obligate him to take the risks of a cop on a dangerous beat. Arguments between the clients inevitably fizzle out on their own, and whatever drug use occurs, he says, he never sees. "You don't see it, you can't tell," he says, referring to drug activity.

The shelter is run by the city, but the forty-eight-year-old Johnson is hired by a private security firm, FJC Securities, Inc., which pays him "a couple of dollars" above the $5.40 an hour that guards working at commercial sites receive. Asked why the guards at public sites receive more money, he grins and nods toward a group of the homeless men who were milling around, as if to say, "There's your answer." But the fact is that government contracts generally require employees to be paid close to union wages, even though Johnson is not in a union. As is true with guards at other security companies, he gets no pension and no health insurance, but he does receive two weeks' paid vacation.

Some people find the men menacing, but Johnson doesn't regard them as threatening at all. They could be his neighbors, he says. In fact, they are. Johnson lives just several blocks away in the heart of Brooklyn's largely black Bedford-Stuyvesant neighborhood, and he walks to work. Clients ask him for money all the time. And he gives them some—a little, anyway. "Quarters, nickels, dimes. There ain't no dollars and stuff like that. They want a quarter, I give 'em a quarter. It ain't nothing but a quarter."

Johnson says that not having medical insurance doesn't bother him. He served in the military in Vietnam, where he saw combat from 1969 to 1971, and he would go to the veterans hospital if he fell ill. "But I ain't never got sick," he says.

Do men often violate the rules inside the shelter? Johnson shrugs inconclusively, and another officer says that guards often see men sleeping together, which is a violation. The guards mostly ignore it. "If you walk in on them in the morning, you just put on the lights and say it's time to go, and that's it," says the officer, whose name is being withheld out of concern that he might be punished for his frank comments. Johnson says the best thing about his job is that it ends when his shift is over. "When I go home, that's it," he says, adding he doesn't think about it again until he arrives the next day.

55. DOORMAN

Salary: About $30,000 a year **Experience or Requirements:** Patience, affability
Hours: 40 a week **Use computer:** No
Benefits: Health, pension, vacation **Workplace:** Entryway of a building
Union: Yes **Risks:** Boredom

For most of his shift, Husnjia Canovic stands at a pulpitlike table near the inner door of the large apartment building at 10 Downing Street. No, not the residence of the British prime minister. It is the home and place of business for some fairly well-off New Yorkers, including a few doctors. They rely on Canovic to direct messengers and to aid residents as they enter and leave with packages, pets, or children. At the age of forty-three, Canovic thinks of himself as a young man, and he wearies of the monotony of the work. "The doorman's job is for old people, for old age," says Canovic, an immigrant from the former Yugoslavia.

His disappointment does not show on his face. Without missing a beat, he interrupts a conversation to listen to a visitor who mentions the name of a tenant. "Make a left. First door on the right." "It's a very busy place," he comments, almost apologetically as he turns his attention back to a discussion of his job. The building is a couple of hundred yards away from the congested streets of Greenwich Village, the heart of which is only a few blocks north. Crime is not a problem here, he says.

Back in his native country, Canovic was an electrician. But he could not do that kind of work here without additional training. He can't afford the time or money for that. "I have to work, because I got three kids and a wife, too," he says. "I don't have time to go to school. I have to pay rent. You need a lot of money. I see a lot of people come here. Get free apartment, free food stamps. I don't have nothing. Here I have to work." A member of a union, Local 32B–32J of the Service Employees International, his salary is set at $14 an hour, giving him a gross weekly salary of $577.33, and take-home of $426.87, he says. He started out with two weeks' paid vacation, but after five years on the job, he now gets three. When he has completed ten years, he will get four weeks. With children aged five, twelve, and seventeen and bills to pay all the time, he assumes he'll be working another twenty-two years, until age sixty-five.

Canovic's two days off are Friday and Saturday, which is not ideal because his wife, who has a nighttime cleaning job at New York University, is off on Saturday and Sunday. "But I sometimes am able to get Sunday off, because my kids like to go to the beach," he says. Driving from his home in Queens, he arrives at 7:00 A.M. every day for work, about an hour early, so that he can find a metered parking space, have coffee, open the doors (which are locked at night because there is no night doorman), and change into his uniform. "I never be late in five years." The parking is one of his biggest headaches. If he is late getting his quarter into the meter, he risks a nice little fine. "Last week I got a ticket, $55."

Before becoming a doorman at 10 Downing Street a year earlier, Canovic was a cleaning man at the building. But then the doorman had a heart attack and management needed a replacement, so they looked to the reliable and personable Canovic. He prefers the cleaning job to the stationary one of being a doorman. But duty called. "All my life I working physically. I work this job one year. Other job is better, I think. I think it's better for young guy, something physical." Then he turns his head toward an approaching lady and says, "Yes? Dr. _____ is first door on your right."

56. GAS STATION ATTENDANT

Salary: About $18,000 a year	**Experience or Requirements:** None
Hours: 66 a week, 5 days	**Use computer:** No
Benefits: None	**Workplace:** Gas station
Union: No	**Risks:** Holdups

James Sica wants to attend the College of Staten Island. College costs money. So Sica has been pumping gas from early in the morning till late at night. Three days a week — Mondays, Wednesdays, and Thursdays — he arrives at seven in the morning at the Mobil service station in downtown Brooklyn near the waterfront and stays until eleven at night. On Tuesdays and Fridays, his schedule is a more regular seven in the morning to four in the afternoon. He's been working that heavy schedule, more than sixty hours a week, for several months; he hopes to lighten up in the fall so he can have more time to study. "In college I would work about forty-five hours, at the most," he says.

Gas-pumping jobs have been diminishing at a meteoric pace as stations have converted to self-service. The remaining pumping jobs, as well as those jobs at self-service places where an employee takes money in a bullet-proof cage, are largely performed by immigrants. Sica, age twenty, is American-born, but he hustles with the energy of any ambitious immigrant. When he's not pumping gas, he is inside the store, which sells snacks and knickknacks for cars. "I'll stock. I'll clean. Restock the refrigerators." One of the things that bothers him most is that there are so many cars coming in for gas that he never has time to sit and eat a hot meal. "That's the worst," he says. "I usually order cold food. Because with hot food I can't eat it hot because I'm always working. You've got to eat in intervals."

From time to time somebody will come in need of help changing a flat tire. That's not really his job, but he's a good guy and he can pick up a few extra dollars. He gets tipped pretty regularly for his gas pumping. "The average is about $1.50 or $2.00, but I'm grateful for anything. Even if it's 10 cents, it's the thought, you know." Told that 10 cents might be considered by some an insult, he smiles and shrugs. "You know, I've had people counting pennies and then giving me a handful of pennies. What can you do? Some people wait for their two cents back."

Even though he's often there alone at night, Sica says he doesn't worry about robberies. "After a certain hour I lock the door, and I come out when a car pulls up," he explains. "That's something everybody in New York has to deal with," he adds, referring to holdups. "And besides, everybody in the neighborhood knows me."

Most days are pretty routine. But every once in a while there's a wise guy who threatens to throw Sica's equilibrium off. "I had a guy come in my face and scream at me," he recalls. "I had just asked him how much gas he needed and, it was weird, he said, 'It's your job to know how much!' I just shut it off and said, 'Have a nice day.' He was cursing me as he was driving away. I can't be arguing with customers in front of customers. I guess he was just having a bad day." The freedom of running a service station without the boss around suits Sica, who wears a tank top shirt, sweatpants, and an earring in one ear.

He thinks he might want to study massage therapy someday. "I like working with my hands....I like working with the public. I like making people feel good. That's me." But in the meantime—and who knows how long that will be?—there are tanks to be filled.

57. INSURANCE SALESWOMAN

Salary: Between $40,000 and $50,000 a year
Hours: 6 to 8 a day, 6 days a week
Benefits: Health, pension, vacation
Union: No

Experience or Requirements: Licenses, based on exams, to sell insurance and mutual funds
Use computer: Yes
Workplace: Cubicle in large office
Risks: Lost sleep after miscommunication with client

Esther Tam likes being financially comfortable, and she likes to chat. So she believes her job selling insurance for Metropolitan Life is ideal. Every workday, Tam tries to convince prospective clients to buy policies paying off large sums of money when policyholders die. She's also busy trying to get the 500 clients who already hold policies with her to purchase bigger ones or to invest in mutual funds backed by Met Life. "For me it's about personal growth, because we are living in a world of finance, and in helping others, I have learned how to invest for myself, so that I can have a good future," says Tam, age forty-two. Since she often goes out to visit her clients and to hunt for prospects, her schedule is flexible; she sometimes works late into the evening and starts late in the morning.

Her job is about building rapport and trust, which means that an idle conversation about the vicissitudes of life, or the joys and pains of work, could lead to an investment. "Like right now, I could be prospecting you," she says with a smile to someone interviewing her about her workday. Tam is under a considerable amount of pressure to add to her list of clients. Every year, she convinces about fifty new people to buy policies from her. The numbers game, which falls in most companies under the rubric of "productivity," bothers Tam more than anything else about her business. Simply adding clients does not necessarily mean that a salesperson is doing what is best for the client, she believes. "I think our success in this field is measured by production many times," she says. "That is important but it might not be the most important. Professionalism is important. Doing your business in the right way, being able to give good advice." She seems pleased, for example, that almost all of her clients have purchased so-called whole life policies, which accrue cash that can later be withdrawn if a crisis arises. "Term" policies, on the other hand, expire when the client is unable to continue making payments, leaving the client with nothing. Once or twice a year Tam loses sleep after a client angrily complains that Tam has not adequately explained some aspect of an investment. Being told by clients that she has let them down in some way, she says, is the most distressing part of the job.

Salespersons are paid commissions based on the total value of policies and how much their clients invest in mutual funds. They get a single check that includes basic salary, plus the commissions. A certain amount is deducted for maintenance of the office. If Tam were to add another twenty hours or so to her weekly schedule, she would be able to make considerably more money. Of the sixteen salespeople in her branch, located on a bustling commercial street in the Flushing section of Queens, a few earn six-figure salaries. But Tam does not aspire to be in those ranks. "I would say at this time one of my goals is to be balanced in this life." After all, she is a person who gave up a promising career as a public school teacher because she simply did not like the job. "I would say that this is easier for me than teaching. It's more interesting because you deal with different people."

Tam drives to work from her home in Queens and uses a parking lot that has what she calls "reasonable" rates. She was born and raised in Hong Kong, and 90 percent of her clients are Chinese, both businesspeople and salaried employees. Retail insurance is essentially an ethnic industry, because "you get along better with people of your own race." She adds, "Of course, there are exceptions, but for most people that is the case."

58. ASSOCIATE ATTORNEY AT A LAW FIRM

Salary: About $130,000 a year
Hours: 9 to 10 a day, 5 days a week, occasional work on weekends
Benefits: Health, 401K retirement plan, vacation
Union: No

Experience or Requirements: College and law school
Use computer: Yes
Workplace: Office with a view of Radio City Music Hall
Risks: None reported

For the best and the brightest young lawyers wanting to "do good" while earning a decent salary, the firm of Paul, Weiss, Rifkind, Wharton & Garrison is about as good as it gets. Twenty-eight-year-old Brian V. Ellner describes himself as a "politically progressive" attorney. In addition to representing some of the firm's paying clients, he also handles a number of "pro bono" cases, in which he works on company time and uses its resources, but does not charge the clients anything. He is working on one case for the New York Civil Liberties Union and two others for gay and lesbian rights groups. As part of his income-producing work, he's litigating an antitrust action, a defamation suit, and a contract dispute.

On a typical weekday, Ellner takes the subway for a ten-minute ride from his home in Chelsea to the offices of Paul, Weiss on the Avenue of the Americas, right near Radio City Music Hall, arriving between nine-thirty and ten o'clock. "I usually go upstairs and get my scrambled egg whites. There's a cafeteria upstairs which we call the jury room. We have sort of a funny name for everything." Back in his office, which has a glass facade with curtains and a clear view to the south, he checks his e-mail, reads the *New York Times,* and gets down to business. Most of the day he reads law books, writes briefs, or prepares for depositions. Sometimes, when he's working a case with other attorneys, he'll gather with them in the conference room. On slow days, when he's not facing an immediate deadline and clients aren't calling continually, he takes his legal reading to a nearby café.

Depositions, which involve questioning witnesses about aspects of a case, can be particularly tedious. "To take a deposition requires a lot [of] work, because you first of all have to be familiar with the entire universe of documents, and out of that universe you have to narrow it down and focus on what you think is most important, what you want to get out of that witness, and from that you create a list of questions, and from that you create a deposition outline." As an associate, he generally reviews his work with a partner or with a senior associate.

The evenings are the most peaceful, if still work-filled, time of day. "Usually after six o'clock, after seven o'clock, work is more solitary. Most people will tell you the best times to get things done at a place like this, unfortunately, are after nine and on a weekend." For a political activist like himself, the law can be a slow and frustrating way to bring about change, says Ellner, a graduate of Dartmouth College and Harvard Law School. Immediately after law school, he traveled through the South and worked on school desegregation cases. He now satisfies his need for political involvement by, among other things, being active with a community board and working on zoning and public safety issues. Paul, Weiss encourages such pursuits, and a number of its attorneys have gone on to seek elective office. Only a small percentage of associates stay more than seven years and become partners, and Ellner assumes he will go into politics someday.

For now, Ellner copes with the pressure of a top law firm by going to the gym, doing yoga, and having what he considers a philosophical view of life. "Sometimes there's a lot on the line," he says, "but it's not the end of the world. It really isn't. People, I think, who have trouble are people who think that it is [the end of the world], three or four times a day. That's a very unhealthy way to live your life."

59. DERMATOLOGIST

Salary: Over $200,000 a year

Hours: At least 12 a day, 5 days a week; fewer hours on remaining days

Benefits: Health, vacation, investment opportunities

Union: No

Experience or Requirements: Medical school

Use computer: Frequently

Workplace: Medical office

Risks: Exposure to viruses and lasers

Roy G. Geronemus specializes in the use of lasers to remove tattoos, scars, wrinkles, and birthmarks and to treat certain skin cancers. Like many doctors in these days of managed care and high technology, he is both a physician and a chief executive officer. Dr. Geronemus, age forty-five, is the director of the Laser and Skin Surgery Center of New York, located on East Thirty-Fourth Street in Manhattan. The center has eighteen treatment tables and a staff of more than sixty people, and it covers two floors of the building it occupies.

He is being interviewed on Veterans Day, which is particularly busy because patients often choose holidays for nonemergency visits. Days like these are a physical and mental strain, even for a man of Geronemus's talent and energy. "I'm here between seven-thirty and eight o'clock [in the morning] every day and I don't leave before seven o'clock [in the evening]. So it's a full day, and I often do bring work home," he says. "I could not do this fifteen years from now at the pace I'm doing it now. I'd have to step back and lessen the demands."

Much of the stress comes from working with anxious patients whose looks may be permanently changed (for the better, he always anticipates) by his handiwork. "You're dealing with permanent outcomes on a patient," he says. "You're making a decision on a daily basis, fifty, one-hundred decisions a day, that can affect someone for life." By his own quick assessment, Geronemus spends about 20 percent of his time managing the business end of the practice, 60 to 70 percent of it with patients, and the remainder working on academic pursuits such as books, articles, and lectures. Being a pioneer in the use of lasers, he says he takes a special delight in seeing the benefits of the treatment. The part of the job he likes best is working with patients. "I delegate a lot of responsibilities," he says, referring to his staff.

As do many other doctors, particularly dermatologists, he complains that he spends an inordinate amount of time convincing insurance companies to pay for his services. Some of his work, such as the removal of wrinkles, might be considered cosmetic and therefore nonreimbursable. But insurance companies sometimes deny payments for necessary operations, because the companies are "just trying to save a few bucks." As for the hazards of his profession, "Certainly one can be exposed to viral things, whether it be hepatitis, HIV, warts." Also, "There are potential injuries to the eyes with lasers." He uses protective wear to shield himself against such dangers.

Geronemus, who lives in Manhattan, graduated from Harvard University with a bachelor's degree in biology in 1975 and then received his medical degree from the University of Miami School of Medicine. He says he has been approached by investors who want to take his business public, a move that would mean a sudden infusion of cash, and also an opportunity to expand and acquire even more equipment. The investment proposals have an attraction for him, Geronemus says, but so far he has not accepted them.

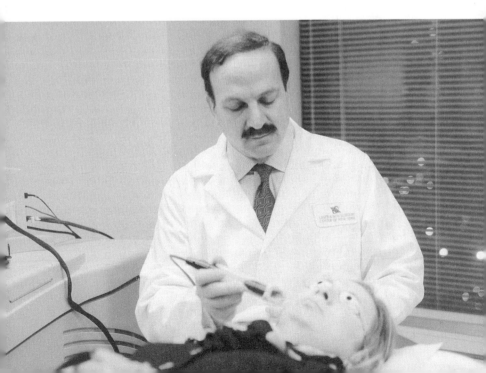

VII. THE FOOD HANDLERS

60. CLAM AND OYSTER SHUCKER

Salary: About $23,600 a year	**Use computer:** No
Hours: 35 a week	**Workplace:** One spot all day in front
Benefits: Health, pension, vacation	of a long table at a restaurant, opening
Union: Yes	shellfish on ice
Experience or Requirements: None	**Risks:** Cuts, muscle pain

Even after twenty years, Felix de Dios still concentrates intensely at his job. First he washes off the crustacean (which could be any of more than 100 different varieties of clams and oysters). Then he sticks his knife into the shellfish, forcing the thin blade from right to left. He throws back the top shell and cuts a muscle of the meat, so that it sits loosely on the bottom shell. All the while, his nostrils are alert for what he says are the extremely rare ones that smell spoiled and can cause someone to get sick. He puts the finished work on a long bed of ice and moves quickly to the next clam or oyster. The whole process takes several seconds.

De Dios is a shucker at the upscale Oyster Bar restaurant in Manhattan. A native of Puebla, Mexico, he reads the orders on computer printouts placed in front of him, and then he gets to work, filling the plate. "I prefer to be quiet because when you're talking you loose 'la onda,'" he says in Spanish, referring to his "wave" or train of thought. "You have to stay quiet." By the day's end he and his two partners have opened 5,000 shellfish, a feat that leaves de Dios's wrists in a numb pain at night that he says he simply shakes off and then forgets about as he falls asleep. "And then the next day I'm ready to go again," he says. Continual movements of the hands such as clam shucking are known to cause repetitive stress injury, but while de Dios acknowledges that even during the day he feels pain, he passes it off as minor. "I just open and close my hands from time to time," he says. He keeps in shape by doing thirty-five push-ups every day, and believes he is healthy.

De Dios is a member of Local 100 of the Hotel Employees and Restaurant Employees Union and he gets two weeks paid vacation a year.

He says he will get a pension through the union but, at age fifty-three, is not thinking of retiring any time in the near future. "I am strong. I plan to keep working."

A large number of unskilled employees at the Oyster Bar are Mexicans. On breaks and sometimes in whispers as they work, they converse in Spanish. They eat lunches specially prepared for the employees, often beef stew or processed turkey or chicken. The shuckers wear yellow gloves to protect themselves from the cuts that happen inevitably from time to time. Oysters are particularly difficult to shuck and require a thinner knife than the one used for clams. "When the oyster is very thick, it can be dangerous because it is more difficult to push the knife through," de Dios says.

Prices for the seafood at the Oyster Bar, located in Grand Central Station, are steep, certainly by blue-collar standards. A dozen clams can cost more than $16 and a combination seafood stew close to $20. De Dios admits to having a taste for seafood. But for him to eat a seafood stew at the Oyster Bar, that's something else again. "I eat seafood, but never here," says de Dios, who lives in uptown Manhattan. "I go to City Island," he says, where the ambience is more homey and the shellfish are cheaper.

61. BAKER

Salary: Under $35,000 a year
Hours: 12 to 14, 6 days a week
Benefits: None
Union: No

Experience or Requirements: Previous job as a baker
Use computer: No
Workplace: Store with pastel colors and Eastern music
Risks: None reported

Inside the storefront on Surrey Place, a quiet commercial strip with a villagelike ambience, Pratibha Agdern is busy baking, or thinking of advertising slogans, or arranging her wares in an attractive way, or kibitzing with customers.

She wants to run a bakery the old-fashioned way. "I think people miss walking into a store and having someone say, 'Hi, Mr. and Mrs. Jones,'" says the forty-seven-year-old Agdern, the manager of Madal Bal Bakery. Having an easy rapport with customers "makes us feel like we're doing something to make their day a little better." There is something ethereal about the look and smell of Madal Bal. The tiles are pink, yellow, and blue. Pictures of the Indian guru Sri Chinmoy line the shop. The scent of scones, croissants, rugelach, and assorted cookies and cakes waft to the nostrils. Agdern tries to capture that old-time European atmosphere that bakeries in New York City once had. It is a feel that has all but died out in the city, she says. She has three full-time employees to assist her in her effort.

Dealing with customers throughout the day has relieved Agdern of much of her natural shyness. "The amazing thing is it's been expanding me as a person," she says. "I feel my creative side is growing. I feel more extroverted. Less shy from dealing with customers." Even on the one day a week when she is not there, Agdern has the bakery on her mind. "On my day off I'm usually doing the books or thinking about advertising," she says. When they have a few moments to think, she and her cohorts attempt to come up with an idea for a new recipe, perhaps a different rugelach (pronounced roo-gah-lah), which is a handrolled pastry, with cheese, chocolate, or nuts inside. "We hope to make one that's just juice sweetened soon, without sugar, with a fruit filling with the consistency almost of jam to give it the flavor you need. We've tried twice but it was not up to par."

The bakery gets so busy around Thanksgiving that they close for two days just so they can work without interruption and meet demand. Christmas is their second busiest season.

Supermarkets, unfortunately, have wooed away customers who once went to the old neighborhood bakers. "In a supermarket, they bake a cookie and dip it in chocolate," she says. "One of our cookies is triple chocolate. It has three kinds of chocolate *in* the dough." The prices of latte and cappuccino are posted in the front of the store.

Agdern had a circuitous route to her current job. She was a psychology major at City College and "my Dad probably wanted me to be a teacher," but she dropped out of college and took jobs as a counselor at a halfway house and then as a statistical clerk. Finally, she found inner peace in the craft of baking. Before becoming manager of Madal Bal she was a baker in a store owned by a friend of hers. She has been baking for a total of thirteen years.

The Madal Bal Bakery is owned by a follower of Sri Chinmoy, and the bakery is lined with books and musical offerings of the spiritual leader. Here and there are photographs of Chinmoy with Princess Diana, Nelson Mandela, and others.

Agdern is also a follower of Chinmoy, and wants the appearance and the smell and the feel of the store to convey a bit of heaven on Earth. The name of the bakery, "Madal Bal," means "heavenly kettle drum" in Sri Chinmoy's native Bengali.

62. FRUIT SELLER

Salary: About $15,000 a year   **Experience or Requirements:** On the job

Hours: 12 a day, 5 days a week   **Use computer:** No

Benefits: None   **Workplace:** Eight feet by four feet of sidewalk

Union: No   **Risks:** None reported

There's no way in the world Ali Muhammed Musa wants this to be his life's work, selling fruits on a street corner. But this is what he's been doing since he immigrated here from Bangladesh in 1997. On the day he is interviewed, Musa is stationed on the bustling northwest corner of Third Avenue and East Thirty-First Street. People pass by, sniff, and—at the rate of several dozen an hour—purchase the clean, sweet-smelling fruit that fairly overflow his stand. The stall is one of several around Manhattan owned by the Turkish immigrant who is Musa's boss.

Musa, twenty-eight, is still struggling with English. "A dollar" is one of his most frequent phrases. Besides saying prices, he mostly listens to his customers' questions, and then obligingly points to the particular fruits they mention. He appears rushed all the time, but manages to give everyone a gentle smile. "All the time busy," he says as he helps a customer pick out apples and bananas, and then searches his pockets for change. He has been doing this twelve long hours a day, five days a week, handling hundreds of dollars per day in cash. On this particular summer day, he is raking in about $60 an hour, which at a steady rate would mean $720 a day or $3,600 a week. He turns the money over to the boss, who drives by several times a day to collect. During these visits, Musa has a chance to have a snack or to use the bathroom across the street at the Tibetan Kitchen.

Recently, Musa, who says he holds an undergraduate degree in the history of art from a college in Bangladesh, was worried that he might soon be out of a job. Mayor Rudolph Giuliani had announced a ban on fruit stands in lower- and mid-Manhattan. But the ban did not materialize. Musa was told his job appeared safe, for the time being. "I get nice work, this is all finished," he says.

Musa knows the English names of all the fruits on his stand: blueberries, strawberries, cantaloupes, seedless golden grapes, mangoes, Holland tomatoes, string beans, broccoli, lemons, cauliflower, bananas, oranges, papaya, and on and on. The metal stand, which is about eight feet by three-and-a-half feet, sits under a blue umbrella. There is a red scale on which he weighs the fruit.

Musa works Monday through Friday. He shares an apartment in Elmhurst, Queens, with five other people.

Throughout the day, he reaches into his left front pocket, which is ever bulging with bills. Possibly because there are always so many people around, no one has ever tried to steal from him, he says. "Fruit, everybody likes," he says in an observation that clearly pleases him.

63. HEAD CHEF AT HEALTH FOOD RESTAURANT

Salary: About $24,000 a year

Hours: 40 a week

Benefits: Health, vacation, profit-sharing plan

Union: No

Experience or Requirements: On the job, previous cooking experience

Workplace: Small area where customers can watch

Risks: Cuts from knives, burns from frying

Keith Lomas arrives at the Perelandra health food emporium and restaurant in Brooklyn Heights at seven-thirty in the morning, and he immediately sets about the task of preparing the meals and desserts that will sit invitingly behind a sloping glass showcase. What he likes most about his job is the creativity it allows him. "I'm always coming up with something new," he says of the menu choices posted every day on the board next to the juice bar. "Usually in the morning I'm cooking about three or four entrees at the same time, and two or three desserts. It gets really hectic at times." On the day he is interviewed, he has prepared a Szechuan tofu meal with green peppers, red peppers, broccoli, and mushrooms; a cashew broccoli concoction; a garlic tofu platter with roast squash, cauliflower, and onions; and a lemon tempeh dish with couscous, cauliflower, corn, squash, string beans, and scallions. For desserts he has made apple cinnamon spice cake, coconut tofu cream pie, and a carrot layer cake.

Lomas, age forty-one, has been working since 1990 at Perelandra, which is located on Remsen Street in Brooklyn Heights. He cooks in an area near the juice bar, and early morning customers coming in for muffins, oatmeal, or tea often watch him admiringly for a few minutes. He enjoys that. As the head chef, Lomas labors alongside a kitchen manager whose job is to prepare the day's soups and casseroles. With them also is a sandwich prep person. By noontime the team must begin serving up the huge pots and platters that will feed 400 customers.

When dicing and slicing, Lomas has learned to be particularly careful. Speed and sharp knives are a dangerous combination. Back when he

started, he cut deep into his thumb and into a nerve. "I was out of commission for three weeks," he says. He still nicks himself from time to time, but the cuts have been minor. Occasionally he burns himself while frying tofu, but he simply treats it with natural oil or cold water.

At the lunch rush, three counter people take orders and serve the customers. As customers line up to purchase their take-out meals, some of them sample an offering, and they generally compliment the cook. That is a high point of Lomas's day. But once in a while, a remark is not so nice, and that sometimes bothers Lomas deeply. "Someone might say, 'You don't know what you're doing,' or 'This doesn't taste good.' You're dealing with the public. Most of the time it's cool, but it can get a bit hairy."

The afternoons, after about 2:00 P.M., are fairly easy. Lomas might browse through the store, looking at the myriad boxes of exotic foods, and he'll try to come up with a new idea for the next day. "That's the fun part of working here," the Brooklyn resident says. "It's a food emporium. You just walk around and say, 'I'll try this and I'll try that,' and you grab this and grab that....I get a chance to express myself creatively. It's not humdrum. You create something, and there's an instant reaction."

64. HEADWAITER

Salary: $25,000 to $32,000 a year, mostly in tips

Hours: 60 to 70 a week, 5 days a week

Benefits: None

Union: No

Experience or Requirements: On the job

Use computer: No

Workplace: A restaurant

Risks: Tired feet

Mark Bermudez thinks people look down on waiters. "They think it is a lowly profession," says Bermudez. "I had a girlfriend that wanted me to change jobs. I said to her, 'But I make twice as much money as you do.'" Bermudez has been working at Gage and Tollner, an old steak and seafood restaurant in downtown Brooklyn, for more than twenty years. He has a master's degree in printmaking and painting but has chosen to remain a waiter. He paints in his few spare hours.

Bermudez learned the haute craft of serving tables in New Orleans, where restaurants and cuisine have an old-world bent. "I was taught very well," he says. "I learned 'French service.' The food is brought out on a silver platter and transferred from one plate to another. You cut the bones out of the meat. You serve from the left and pour from the right. At Gage and Tollner, the service is more casual." The dining room at Gage and Tollner is divided into four workstations, one for each waiter on the shift. All of them are men, and forty-four-year-old Bermudez is the chief. He works two shifts a day, five days a week, starting at ten-thirty in the morning and staying until ten-thirty at night, sometimes later.

At Gage and Tollner, waiters take the orders, but the main courses are brought from the kitchen by "runners." The job of the waiter is fairly genteel. "The waiter gets the drinks, gives the patrons the wine list, serves dessert, and serves coffee. I see myself as the general camp counselor. I oversee the general well-being of the guests." Part of being a good waiter, he says, is knowing when to try to engage the guests in conversation and when to leave them alone. In general, they prefer to be left to themselves, he has learned.

Bermudez says many people come into the restaurant and ask to be served by him. That's in part because he makes it a point to remember the names of the guests, which makes them feel special. "When you bring people into the restaurant and the waiter knows your name, it makes an impression."

Gage and Tollner opened in 1879. It has oil paintings, wood paneling, and gas lamps hanging from the ceiling.

The worst days for Bermudez are those when the boss is angry. "There is no real danger on the job, except when you disagree with the boss," he says. "It is a bad day when you have the boss upset with you, yelling at you for something you've done wrong or haven't done."

The greater part of his earnings by far is in tips, his regular salary from the establishment being only about $25 a day. The restaurant is busiest from October through December. Things slow down in January, then pick up again in the spring. "The hours are long," says Bermudez, who travels to work by subway from his residence in Brooklyn. "I basically never sleep. I stay up late and I get up early. I drink a lot of coffee." He stays with the job, he says, because "I enjoy making sure that people have a good time."

65. RABBI, SUPERVISING WORLDWIDE INSPECTIONS OF KOSHER FOODS

Salary: Above $60,000 a year

Hours: 45 a week, excluding religious duties

Benefits: Health, investment plan, vacation

Union: No

Experience or Requirements: Rabbinical studies, years of experience studying the food industry

Use computer: Yes

Workplace: An office and occasionally restaurants around the world

Risks: None reported

Rabbi Moshe Elefant supervises hundreds of rabbis around the world who certify food as kosher. At the main office in Manhattan of the Orthodox Union (O.U.), he is Executive Rabbinic Coordinator of the Kashruth Division. Kashruth is the Hebrew term for kosher. "O.U., by far, is the largest kosher food certification agency in the world," Elefant says. "I would say 70 percent of the food (in the world) that is kosher is O.U.–certified."

Elefant, who is forty years old, spends most of the day in his threadbare office, talking on the phone with affiliated rabbis, restaurant owners, food plant managers, and Jewish consumers who have questions about kosher products. He reads and replies to constant streams of e-mail and faxes. He also has regular meetings with his staff to discuss recent developments in the food production industry and to determine how those changes affect their work. From time to time he travels, visiting between thirty and forty food establishments a year in the United States and abroad, observing them and checking on the work of the *Mashgim*, as the rabbinical inspectors are known in Hebrew. The work is of critical importance to hundreds of thousands of Orthodox Jews who follow Mosaic law, which prohibits the eating of pork and the mixing of dairy and meat products, among other things. "It's certainly a sin to eat nonkosher," Elefant says. "It's a violation of what we know is God's will, and obviously it comes with its repercussions....It's not within my nature to tell you how God will react to someone's doing what He doesn't want. God will do His job and we are here to do our job."

Some *Mashgim* are stationed full-time at restaurants or plants. Others are itinerant, and still others live in far-flung places and are paid on a per-diem basis to inspect local establishments. In the United States, a full-time *Mashgiach*, which is the singular term for *Mashgim*, earns between $55,000 and $60,000 a year. Elefant says his salary is above that, but not significantly so. Technically, any rabbi is qualified to be a *Mashgiach*, but practically speaking it takes "years and years" of dealing with the food industry to perform the job adequately. "The food industry is a very dynamic science, and we're constantly learning new things. Getting that knowledge of food technology is crucial to doing my job properly. We have constant in-house conferences, to increase knowledge." He says he is currently looking into the issue of canned vegetables, which were once considered inherently kosher. "What we find is that in some cases they're processing the vegetables, but they're also canning (nonkosher) meat and, for lack of a better word, contaminating the equipment."

In addition to his hours at work, Elefant spends time performing religious duties outside the office. "I wake up every morning at 4:00 A.M., because I give a lecture every morning on the Talmud at a synagogue where I live in Brooklyn, in Borough Park. I prepare the lecture and give it at five-thirty. And at six-thirty I pray. All Jewish males are required to pray three times a day in a quorum." A quorum, he explains, is ten males above the age of thirteen. He then returns home to have breakfast, after that taking the subway to his office on Seventh Avenue. He has been working at his job for eleven years. In observance of the Sabbath, employees at the Orthodox Union leave work shortly after noon on Fridays, and return on Monday. "I arrive here at nine-thirty and stay to five-thirty. I've never taken a lunch break yet."

66. DISHWASHER

Salary: About $17,500 a year   **Experience or Requirements:** None
Hours: 10 a day, 6 days a week   **Use computer:** No
Benefits: Vacation   **Workplace:** A kitchen
Union: No   **Risks:** Cuts

Guillermo Perez works at the Dojo West Restaurant just on the edge of the campus of New York University in Greenwich Village. The crowd of young customers is pretty much nonstop. They are drawn by the quick, no-frills service and the relatively economical prices. Morning to night, the place is hopping.

Perez smiles a lot, even though he works all day on his feet, scraping and washing plates, cutting carrots and potatoes. He also scrubs the walls of the huge kitchen when he's not doing anything else. Perez's bosses love him, and have even encouraged him to try for the higher-paying job of cook. But that requires learning some English, so he can understand the waiters, and a little Chinese, in order to communicate with the other cooks. He's satisfied, for the time being, doing what he's doing. "The truth is, nothing bothers me about this work," he says in Spanish. "I like it here. I am very comfortable."

Perez has little time for leisure activities in his life, and he looks forward to Sunday, his only day off, a chance to rest and romp. "That is *futbol* day," he says, using the term for soccer. He and friends gather at a park to play the game or to watch a match on television. Perez is thirty-two and has been in the States for three years. The manager of the Dojo West says he often helps immigrant employees like Perez who might be having problems with the Immigration and Naturalization Service.

Perez and his co-workers don't care about not having health insurance. In their twenties and thirties, they are not feeling sick and are not expecting to get sick. Rent is not a problem, Perez says, because he lives in Flushing, Queens, with three others who kick in with him for the $650 a month. He saves on the cost of food, he says, by eating just about all of his meals at the Dojo.

Of course, he would prefer the status of his old job in Puebla, Mexico—installing aluminum windows. He did that for wages, a few piddling pesos, but what he really wants to do is have his own window installation business. He concludes that it takes money to make money. "If there you can earn a dollar, here you earn ten dollars. It's as simple as that," he says. And so he never regretted paying $2,000 to a coyote (smuggler) to take him to Los Angeles three years ago, where he stayed for a year, working where he could for $280 to $300 a week. Now in New York, he sends some money regularly to his wife and two sons back in Mexico. But he's saving the greater part of his earnings so that he can accumulate $20,000 and return to Mexico to open that business installing windows. He thinks he is about a year away from his goal. Perez gets two weeks' paid vacation a year, but he chooses to stay and work for the extra money.

67. DIM SUM WORKER

Salary: About $10,200 a year **Experience or Requirements:** Years on the job
Hours: 40 a week, when employed **Use computer:** No
Benefits: Strike benefits **Workplace:** Restaurants
Union: Yes **Risks:** Abusive restaurant owners

A dim sum woman pushes her wheeled cart filled with tasty-looking appetizers, winding her way through the Chinese restaurant as customers look and choose. On her tray are specialties such as harkow (shrimp dumplings) and siu mai (pork dumplings). For several years, until 1997, forty-year-old Fung Chew was a dim sum worker with the Silver Palace Restaurant on the Bowery in Chinatown. Of the scores of local eating places that attract tens of thousands of diners a week, the Silver Palace was the only one that had a union staff, according to Chew and organizers at Restaurant Workers Union on Catherine Street in Chinatown. The working conditions there were relatively good. She and co-workers did not have to follow the custom of paying their bosses for their jobs. And she was not forced to work out of her job classification.

But in May of 1997 the restaurant closed. A new owner reopened it as the New Silver Palace in August but would not permit his employees to be members of the union. Employees at first did not know how to respond. Chew explains through a translator: "Had I gone up there, the job would have been one without security. How would I raise a family? I am a single mother, with two little kids. That kind of working condition is not for humans." So she and her co-workers met and complained to the owner, and they were eventually locked out. They have been regularly picketing the closed restaurant for months.

Chew has tried to work at other restaurants in the area—those that were willing to hire striking Silver Palace workers. But the jobs were more difficult than she was used to. In addition to doing dim sum work, she had to "clean the place and wash pans and dishes." She earned about $850 a month and got no tips, compared to the $1,200 a month she was getting back at the Silver Palace. She eventually stopped working at the nonunion places and began collecting unemployment compensation until she

exhausted those payments; by the end of the summer of 1998 she was receiving strike benefits of about $800 a month from her union.

Women are accepted as dim sum workers but generally not as waiters. In 1994, Chew says, a dim sum woman was promoted to waitress at the Silver Palace, and there was a huge uproar. All the men complained. She laughs at the tale. Asked why there are no dim sum men, she smiles and shrugs. That's the way it is. There's men's work and there's women's work. In the garment business, for another example, the men tend to do the buttons and press the garments, she points out. All she cares about is fair pay and decent treatment, says Chew, who immigrated to New York from the People's Republic of China in 1979.

VIII. THE TRANSPORTERS

68. HORSE-DRAWN CARRIAGE DRIVER

Salary: About $18,000 a year
Hours: 10:00 A.M. to 6:00 P.M., 6 to 7 days a week
Benefits: None
Union: No

Experience or Requirements: Love of horses, licenses from consumer affairs and health departments
Use computer: No
Workplace: Central Park
Risks: Aggressive bus drivers

Anita McGill parks her horse-drawn buggy, which she lovingly calls the Pink Cadillac, outside the Tavern on the Green restaurant on the west side of Central Park. Then she waits in a line of half-a-dozen carriages that one by one will take customers on twenty-minute rides around the park. Celebrities often ride with McGill. Some of them, like Paul Simon, ask for her regularly; and Marla Maples, ex-wife of Donald Trump, also goes out with her on occasion. Maples is a good tipper, "but she talks on her cell phone all the way around," the thirty-year-old McGill says.

The side-to-side rocking of the carriage as the horse trots along is invigorating. And even in the thick of noisy Manhattan traffic, McGill can engage in pleasant conversation with her passengers. Owning a hansom and horse is no pushcart operation. Because they date back to the days when they were a primary means of transport, hansoms have a legal status similar to yellow taxicabs, with "medallions," or licenses, that are worth thousands of dollars. Add to that the cost of the carriage, about $12,000, and the horse, about $2,000, and you've got a nice little enterprise. McGill owns her own carriage and two horses, but she works out of a stable on the West Side owned by her parents and uses their license. She generally works six or even seven days a week, and she charges $34 for the twenty-minute ride.

Most carriage drivers are immigrants who come from places like Turkey and Ireland. "They're from countries that use horses on a regular basis, not as a luxury item," McGill says. Full-time drivers like McGill can earn between $350 and $400 a week, depending on a number of factors, including weather. McGill is from an immigrant Irish family, and the tradition of working with horses remains. Her dad, in fact, is a retired civilian employee of the New York City Police Department who used to take care of the department's horses.

For McGill, the job is about freedom, people, and, of course, horses. "This is Captain," she says, referring to the nine-year-old Morgan pulling her carriage. She also has a horse named Brandy. "There's not a day I don't want to come out to work," says McGill. She's been driving now for ten years. The best days of the year for hansom cab drivers are Mother's Day and Thanksgiving, because families want to be together on the town. There are bad days, too. Because popping firecrackers can spook a nervous horse, the Fourth of July can be dangerous. McGill doesn't work on the Fourth.

It takes about three weeks of training to learn to be a carriage driver, McGill says. Many drivers like the work because they can do it seasonally and according to their own schedule. McGill knows drivers who are teachers, actors, and even one who's a funeral director. As a student years ago attending Fashion Industries High School, McGill did well in interior decoration and thought that would be her life's work. But "then when I started driving I didn't want to do anything else." Of course, much of her work is standing around waiting for customers. And occasionally chauffeurs argue over who gets which customer. McGill says that some drivers become envious when prospective riders insist on going in her distinctive pink carriage. Children especially love the color, she says. There are dangers to watch for in the streets also. "Buses are known to sweep over in front of the horse all the time, impatient to get past you," she says. And occasionally, motorists yell at her angrily. "The biggest comment I hear is, 'You belong in the park!'"

69. BIKE MESSENGER

Salary: $35,000 a year
Hours: 12 a day, 5 days a week
Benefits: None
Union: No

Experience or Requirements: Must be in good physical condition
Use computer: No
Workplace: Streets and sidewalks of the city
Risks: Aggressive drivers of motor vehicles

Time is always of the essence for Fernando Rivera (just call him "The Kid") as he speeds along the streets of Manhattan on his 1994 Cannondale high-speed bicycle, delivering messages and packages for Gregory's Messenger Service. He wears a Nike bandanna to absorb the sweat and, one presumes, because it's stylish. He carries on his back a $125 waterproof tote bag. Rivera gets paid a commission for every item he delivers. He says that "elite" riders like him—those who have proven themselves to be reliable over a number of years—receive 55 percent of the charge for each item. Others might get 50 percent. "And at some companies if you miss a day of work, they cut you 5 percent, down to 45," he says.

Having no benefits such as sick time, he tries never to miss work. He can recall only once in his six years with Gregory's that he was very ill. He had a case of pneumonia, and even that didn't stop him, he says. "I needed to make that money so I rode it out of my system, drank a lot of water."

Rivera, age thirty-three, is a tough New Yorker, but he fears the following things: summer, winter, and Halloween.

In the summertime he sweats profusely and tries to drink water constantly. Good-hearted customers note his discomfort. "They might offer you a cup of water or a soda to show their gratitude. It makes you feel better," he says. "Then you've got people who don't give a shit. They just don't care." But the winter, now that's even more challenging. "In the winter you have to have the proper gear," he says, referring to heavy clothing and wraps. "The company don't provide none of that. That's what separates the men from the boys, the winter." On Halloween, especially at night, bike riders risk being pelted with eggs as they cruise the streets. "The only day I don't like to ride home is Halloween." On Halloween, he carries his bicycle on the subway to get to and from work.

A typical bike messenger, according to Rivera, makes $15,000 to $16,000 a year. He says he makes the relatively bounteous salary of $35,000 because he is extremely ambitious and has a boss who appreciates him. Some days he even helps with administrative chores in the office, taking calls and such. "I deserve what I get," he says. "I take a lot of spills. I would get up, bleeding, and still deliver packages. God blessed me with the boss I have now.... I busted my ass to get where I'm at."

Rivera worries that he may not have enough to help adequately with the education and other needs of his two daughters. He wants to begin saving, for them, and also so that when he gets older he can start a little business. It doesn't matter too much what kind; perhaps a little grocery store. "I know people who've been messengers for fifteen, twenty years, and they ain't got nothing to show for it." But as he sees it now, he's got many years to go, so he'd better stay in shape. He stretches and exercises every morning, getting ready for the sixty miles a day he covers on his bike. He also stays in shape because New York is a rough city, and there are street guys who will steal from a messenger if they can. "Some people know who they can fuck with," he says. "I have no problems."

70. "SPOTTER" WHO TOWS CARS WITH OUTSTANDING TICKETS

Salary: About $30,000 a year, including overtime	**Experience or Requirements:** Typing, ability to drive tow truck
Hours: 9 a shift; generally 1 shift a day, 5 days a week	**Use computer:** Yes
Benefits: Vacation	**Workplace:** Streets of the city
Union: No	**Risks:** Angry vehicle owners

Nelson Hernandez drives around in a tow truck looking for vehicles with unpaid tickets. When he finds one he quickly, almost furtively, hooks it up to his truck and hauls it away for keeping in his company's lot. It stays there until the owner comes and pays the outstanding fines. Hernandez, age thirty-four, works for R & D Towing, and he's called a "spotter." He knows he is a hateful man to many New Yorkers. Often as he's driving around they let him know it by shouting obscenities at him. Car owners consider the city's parking fines—which start at $55 in midtown—to be cruel and unusual punishment, and the inconvenience and expense of the towing only adds to their fury. Typically they pay several hundred dollars, often much more, to get their vehicles back. But Hernandez says he's only doing his job. He also enjoys the hunt.

One summer day finds him cruising the East Side of Manhattan. As always, he carries with him two computers. One of them is a palmtop attached by Velcro to his steering wheel. As he drives along the streets, he punches in the license plate numbers, one after another. If the palmtop indicates a car has more than $230 in unpaid tickets—making it fair game for towing—Hernandez enters the plate into a larger computer sitting to his right and attached by a cord to the cigarette lighter. Information about the owner pops up on the larger computer. "At the end of the day I might have typed in 2,000 plates into the palmtop," Hernandez says. "I might get ten, or I might not get 'jack' that day." He gets paid a straight salary, but his company, R & D, works under contract with city marshals, who do get paid according to the number of vehicles taken.

Hernandez is not out there by himself. He is part of a team of several others, including a marshal. The marshal generally rides with a chauffeur who more often than not is a retired New York City police officer. In their separate cars, the members of the team are always near each other and in radio contact. Finally, bingo. A car above the $230 limit of outstanding tickets! Hernandez is delighted. He quickly hooks the maroon Mercury Grand Marquis to his tow truck as the marshal's driver blocks traffic, and the marshal, with his badge hanging from a chain around his neck, stands by on guard. "You don't want any confrontation," Hernandez says later. "You don't know what you'll get into.... You want to be in and out in thirty seconds. And thirty seconds is too much." Hernandez drops the car off at a "staging area" on a sparsely populated city block, about a half mile away. Later in the day, a "transporter" from R & D Towing will come and haul it to the company's lot in Brooklyn. "One guy once threw a punch at me, but the marshal got in between us, Hernandez says. You don't want to start brawling. But sometimes it just goes with the territory."

Hernandez starts his day at 6:30 A.M. He works straight to 3:00 P.M., and doesn't take a lunch or coffee break. Instead he usually grabs a sandwich and eats on the run. Hernandez has no health insurance or pension plan but gets two weeks' paid vacation around Christmastime. "If you get hurt on the job, the boss, he'll take care of you and do the right thing," Hernandez says. "As far as sick days, we don't have sick days like a regular employer might give you, but if you don't feel well, you stay home and relax. You do lose a day's pay, but he'll try to make it up, give you a night tour, so you can keep that pace and earn the same salary."

71. CIRCLE LINE
TOUR GUIDE

Salary: $15,000 a year, generally between May and October

Hours: About 45 a week, in season

Benefits: Health, pension, vacation

Union: Yes

Experience or Requirements: Background in theater is helpful, but not mandatory

Use computer: No

Workplace: Hudson and East Rivers

Risks: Bad weather, people tossing objects from shore

David Wayne Parker punches a clock upon arriving to work. Then he changes into his white naval officer's uniform. He is one of about a dozen tour guides with the Circle Line, which operates boats of various sizes that cruise up and down Manhattan Island. Parker and the other guides are actors who have found a certain glamour, and a paycheck, in performing for tourists on the water for an enjoyable afternoon or evening. The longest tour offered by Circle is a three-hour trip around the whole island.

Guides are proud of the "spiels" they give during the tours, and they shamelessly steal lines from one another. Some turn the whole trip into a seamless story about the history and people of New York, including landmarks such as the Statue of Liberty, the World Trade Center, and the Empire State Building. And they must always be ready to weave local current events into their presentation. They read the city newspapers, looking for fresh material. One routine that the thirty-six-year-old Parker maintains no one else can do is his impersonation of the main character from the old television program *Gilligan's Island*. Telling riders he is about to do Gilligan in a hurricane, he grabs a pole and holds himself absolutely horizontal, looking for all the world like a human flag in the wind. The crowd shows its pleasure with applause. As he passes Ellis Island, Parker often breaks into an anecdote about a man and woman who arrived from Eastern Europe as immigrants more than eighty years ago. At the end, he somberly informs his audience that the couple he described were his great-grandparents. People are often teary after the telling.

Bad times on the water include squalls that come up suddenly and make for scary trips. And then there was the occasion some years back when a sniper shot at the boat and wounded a tourist. Parker was working on that boat, he says.

In order to get his job, Parker had to audition in front of the "pier manager" and a couple of other guides. Candidates are asked to read a tour spiel about one of the many sights on the Circle Line tours. Openings are few because most of the guides have been with Circle for "double digit" years, says Parker, and they have no intention of leaving voluntarily. Parker has been a guide since 1994. He worked at the snack bar before that. Unfortunately, the employment is highly seasonal, and Parker generally works only about six months or so out of the year, with most of his hours crammed into the spring, summer, and early fall. He takes two buses and the subway to get to the Circle Line (at Forty-Second Street and the Hudson River in Manhattan) from his home in the Red Hook section of Brooklyn.

One of the biggest drawbacks of his position, Parker concedes, is the pay, which some would say does not meet his level of education. (Parker has a master's degree in fine arts.) In off-peak months, Parker must support himself doing other things, such as phone surveys of business executives for *Institutional Investor* magazine. By his own description, he is naturally shy, but he loves the job and hopes to keep doing it. "It's like someone saying, 'Dave, we need you to volunteer to do a job and be out in the sun and meet people from all over the world, and some of them will be beautiful women, who will be single. You will have to entertain them for two to three hours at a stretch.' And I say, 'Okay, twist my arm.'"

72. ILLEGAL PASSENGER VAN DRIVER

Salary: $10,500 a year, minus tickets and other fines

Hours: 12 or more a day, 7 days a week, except when the van is confiscated

Benefits: None

Union: No

Experience or Requirements: Driver's license

Use computer: No

Workplace: City streets

Risks: Summonses, friskings, and alleged beatings by police

Reg Martin—not his real name—drives his van up and down Flatbush Avenue, swinging over to the side of the street when someone waves to get his attention. Martin then pulls the rope attached to the passenger door, letting the person enter, and proceeds along his route. As he drives, he holds a two-way radio, which keeps him in touch with other van drivers who, like him, shuttle between downtown Brooklyn and the borough's far reaches to the south, near the Kings Plaza shopping mall. His nickname, or radio "handle," is Star Two.

There are hundreds of such illegal "dollar vans" operating largely in Brooklyn and Queens. The drivers say they are providing a service necessitated by the paucity of city buses in minority neighborhoods. And the city has in fact licensed a small percentage of them. But authorities say the illegal vans do not have adequate insurance and have not gone through the stringent inspection process required of public vehicles. Plus, the vans are siphoning thousands of riders from the city buses. And so Martin is constantly looking out for police, who in some precincts have cracked down hard on the drivers. On the day he is interviewed, Martin's van is idle. Too many plainclothes policemen out looking for people like him, he says. "It's been getting worse now, because now they're chasing people in vans." In Brooklyn, there have been a number of serious accidents caused when dollar van drivers were being pursued by police.

Complaints of police harassment of the drivers abound. A week earlier, Martin says, police officers in plain clothes approached his van. "One of them said, 'Get the fuck out the car!'...So the guy jumped on the step [of the van] and grabbed my clothes and tried to pull me through the window, punching me. No uniform. Didn't show me nothing at all. You see these marks here, that's where he hit me with the radio." He says he was arrested and charged with resisting arrest and reckless endangerment. Most often, drivers are given summonses, occasionally as many as fifteen at a time. Sometimes the vans are confiscated and they have to pay upwards of $1,000 in penalties and back summonses to get their vehicles back, Martin says. Like most other van drivers, Martin, age forty-one, is an immigrant from the English-speaking Caribbean. He says he owns his van, and each month he lays out $699 for insurance, $764 for loan payments, and $200 for gas. He nets about $350 in a week if he drives the whole seven days. When he can, he tries to get transporting jobs on the side. "You may get someone who wants to move some furniture, or a group that wants to take a trip to Great Adventure." He says he has been driving a dollar van for three years, but is not sure how much longer he can continue, given the risks. "I may go back out tomorrow," he says.

73. CITY BUS DRIVER

Salary: About $57,000 for the year, including overtime

Hours: 57 a week, including 17 hours overtime

Benefits: Health, pension, vacation

Union: Yes

Experience or Requirements: A civil service test, high school equivalency, Class B driver's license

Use computer: No

Workplace: The streets of Queens

Risks: None reported

Sure, sometimes the teenagers get a little out of hand, and every once in a while a passenger seems determined to start an argument. But Arrie Parker says driving a bus for the New York City Transit Authority is the best job he's ever had. And he's had a few. "This job, you can pick your working hours and how you want to work," he says. "You [get to] pick by seniority." The downside, many other drivers would argue, is that the days are long and spent in a seat, not the greatest thing for the spine.

Parker, fifty-nine, is a twelve-year veteran. He shows up for the 7:03 to 8:41 A.M. rush-hour trip between Hollis and Queens Village in Queens, and then he takes off for the next several hours, making the brief drive to his home just across the border on Long Island, where he has breakfast and runs errands. Then he returns to Queens to begin a 12:52 P.M. round-tripper, and he does two more "trippers" to finish his day. The schedule gives him seventeen hours of overtime a week, boosting his salary by more than $10,000 a year. But perhaps more than anything else, he says, he cherishes the permanence of a civil service job like his. "I love the job security," he says. "You don't have to worry about being laid off."

The TA has a "25-55" rule, he says. An employee can retire with a pension after twenty-five years on the job or (assuming he's passed the ten-year vesting mark) at the age of fifty-five. "If I could start over again, when I came to New York in '58, if I could have gotten on the TA then, I'd be retired already," he says, smiling dreamily at the thought.

Parker is an easygoing type who says he never gets into arguments with passengers. "I'm from North Carolina, down south. Down south, you always get plenty of breeding and manners. Most Southerners are like that—kind and considerate." He is talking while making his run

from the Queens Village depot to his end-of-the-line stop in Hollis. He applies the brakes gently as a group of passengers exits from the front. "Thank you," they say, almost in unison as they begin stepping down. Parker nods and smiles.

In contrast to this one, his job of twenty-seven years as a supervisor at a food company was full of headaches. "I had eight guys working under me," he says of the food company. "It's always difficult with people under you. They call in and say they can't come in." Over the years he's also been a security guard and a real estate agent.

Looking at his side mirror and turning the steering wheel, he pulls off on another afternoon run. He says he feels healthy and happy. "In this job, I only have to worry about me," he says.

74. CLASSIC CAR SALESMAN

Salary: $75,000 to $125,000 a year

Hours: 9:00 A.M. to 6:00 P.M. Monday through Friday; 11:00 A.M. to 3:00 P.M. Saturday

Benefits: Health, vacation

Unions: No

Experience or Requirements: Previous experience in car sales; knowledge of history of classic cars

Use computers: Yes

Workplace: Dealership showroom

Risks: A bad economy

The classic car dealership where Ray Agcaoili works as co-manager is sandwiched between the artsy Soho neighborhood and Manhattan's financial district. People, young and swimming in money from a long-running Wall Street boom, stroll in throughout the day to look around. Without any coddling, they have been known to plop down a bundle of money on a vehicle that catches their fancy. "A young person, like twenty-six, he worked with the New York Stock Exchange, he came and purchased a '72 Jaguar, at the beginning of this month. It was high forty thousand. He paid with a certified check." Agcaoili smiles at the memory.

Agcaoili, thirty-six years old and an immigrant from the Philippines, started out working in computer network administration, local area networks, and such. But he felt cooped up, surrounded by whirring machines. And what's more, the money wasn't as good as he's getting now at 180 Sports Classics. Plus, he loves talking to people and being around cars. Agcaoili has immersed himself in the history and minutiae of the Ferraris, Jaguars, and Mercedes Benzes that he sells.

Slightly after closing time on a summer's day, Traci Godfrey, an actress who lately has been doing voice-overs for television commercials, knocks on the glass door. Agcaoili lets her in and shows her two convertibles, and he pleasantly answers her questions about mileage and price. Godfrey and her friend admire the vehicle for about fifteen minutes, thank Agcaoili, and then leave. "We cater to a select clientele," says Agcaoili, who drives to work in his Mercedes from his home in Hoboken, New Jersey. To reinforce the point, he opens his drawer and displays the business cards inside. They are from people with Smith, Barney and other firms.

Agcaoili likes to talk about the car that once belonged to Evita Perón. "It was a 1949 Cisitalia, and it went for $125,000," he says. "At the beginning of the year we sent it to Italy." A 1995 Humvee—the military jeep brought to popular attention during the Persian Gulf War—sits on the narrow lot of the dealership at 180 West Broadway. A new Hummer, as Humvees are sometimes called, can sell in the "high eighties," he says. The one on the lot sold for about $50,000.

Sometimes the salesmen at 180 Sports Classics sell cars without even opening their mouths. That's because 180 Sports Classics is on the Internet. Recently someone keyed the words "Porsche" and "Cabriolet" onto the Web site and liked what he saw. The Internet surfer bought the car for $39,000.

75. HARBOR PILOT

Salary: $150,000 a year

Hours: 8 a day, 5 days a week
as association president,
maybe 60 hours a week if piloting

Benefits: Health, pension, vacation
through Pilots' Association

Union: Yes

Experience or Requirements: Bachelor's degree;
aptitude test, interview

Use computer: Yes

Workplace: New York Harbor

Risks: Falling into the sea

On a typical workday, a harbor pilot receives a call telling him a ship is waiting to be taken out to sea. The pilot then goes to the harbor where the vessel is waiting and he boards it. It is the pilot's job to steer big ships safely through the narrow, congested waters of New York Harbor, all the way out to sea. "You get to handle the largest moveable man-made objects in the world," says fifty-five-year-old William Sherwood of Staten Island, a harbor pilot since 1964.

But once a pilot steers a boat into the ocean, his job is done, and he has to turn the boat over to its captain. And how does he leave the ship? By climbing down fifty feet of rope into a launch that is rising and falling with the waves. This descent from the ship is the most dangerous part of the work. Sherwood has never fallen in, but a couple of years ago a pilot did fall "and was damn near dismembered," Sherwood recalls. Once he is safely in the waiting launch, the pilot is taken to Pilot Station, a special ship where he waits for his next assignment: an arriving vessel. And just as he previously climbed *down* the departing ship, he will now climb *up* this one and steer it *into* New York Harbor.

Eighty-four pilots currently work out of the Sandy Hook Pilots' Association, and they are regulated by the states of New York and New Jersey. The pilots are private contractors, each of whom owns a share in the association. Sherwood has been the president of the association for the past four years, and spends most of his time these days working out of the group's main office on Staten Island. Because he serves year to year at the pleasure of the members, he could soon be back at sea—which would not bother him at all. "I miss it because the thing that has always made it interesting to me is that there are no regular hours." Pilots work in shifts, spending anywhere from eighteen to thirty hours at a stretch steering ships and waiting at the Pilot Station for the next assignment. They get 56 days off for every year they work.

Sherwood feels the sea is in his blood, and this work has the added advantage of keeping him relatively close to home, unlike merchant seamen and others who spend months away on the water. Pilots gross up to $150,000 a year, out of which they pay for Social Security, retirement, medical insurance, and equipment. Sherwood estimates that $33,000 goes toward such expenses. It used to be that virtually the only way to become a pilot was to know one, Sherwood says. He argues that this has been changing, but none of the 84 pilots is a woman or a minority. Those interested in becoming a pilot's apprentice must be physically fit, have a bachelor's degree, pass an aptitude test, and go through an interview by a six-member panel. Applicants must also be under the age of twenty-seven.

Pilots get to meet interesting people on the vessels they steer. "You deal almost exclusively with foreign ships, so you often get a very international flavor for world politics," Sherwood says. "You know everything that you read in the newspapers has got an inevitable American spin on it. Very different when you talk to these people."

76. LIMOUSINE CHAUFFEUR

Salary: $75,000 a year, gross
Hours: 12 to 14 a day,
5 to 6 days a week
Benefits: None
Union: No

Experience or Requirements: Limousine license
Use computer: No
Workplace: Limousine, the streets of the city
Risks: None reported

"I make more money driving a limo than any work I've ever done," Taylor Laguerre says. Laguerre, who is forty-three, went through three years of college, dropped out, and then tried a series of jobs, including one as manager of a restaurant at a popular hotel. Then he decided he had enough money to make payments on a top-of-the-line Lincoln. He signed a contract with Carey Limousine service, and now he drives the rich and famous or anyone else willing to pay $131.25 for an hour and a half of his services. Some of his passengers are regulars. They contact him directly or they call Carey and ask for him. Among those who have requested him on trips to New York, he says, is Carol Moseley-Braun, the former U.S. senator from Illinois. He also has driven regularly for top diplomats who appreciate his alertness and his ability to maneuver his long vehicle easily through heavy traffic. Drivers at Carey tend to be ambitious immigrants who are savvy and polished enough to get along with the folks who run things at the limousine company, Laguerre says. He himself came to the United States as a youngster with his parents from Haiti. Most of the drivers with Carey, he says, are Europeans, largely Russians.

"Our top drivers make $140,000 a year," he says, but he has not yet made over $75,000 in his twelve years on the job. Because Carey chauffeurs are in essence contractors, they have to keep good business records. And for Laguerre and other drivers, that is by far the most tedious part of their work. The tallying begins even before the employment does. A prospective driver needs about $6,000 up front as a deposit to begin working with the company, and he or she must also have a good credit rating. As with any business, there are regular expenses such as a couple of thousand dollars in monthly fees, including payments for the radio connection to the home base and a car phone.

Laguerre enjoys wheeling through traffic and feels spiffy standing next to his late-model limousine in his black chauffeur's uniform. He doesn't particularly like those hours between appointments when he's just waiting for a phone call or for the unlikely chance that some wealthy, or desperate, person will wave a wad of hundreds in front of him and say he needs to be driven around the city. But he says he has no intention of changing careers.

77. FERRY BOAT DECKHAND

Salary: About $30,000 a year	**Experience or Requirements:** Experience on boats
Hours: 13 a day, 4 days a week	**Use computers:** No
Benefits: Health, pension, and vacation	**Workplace:** New York Harbor
Union: No	**Risks:** None reported

Grant Albright likes to say he's in the urban transportation business. But he has nothing to do with buses or subways. Albright, age forty, is the senior deckhand on the Express II, a ferry that carries commuters between New Jersey and downtown Manhattan. He cleans and maintains the boat, and collects tickets from up to 500 passengers a day.

"With most jobs on boats, you're away," Albright says. "You're away sometimes months at a time. But the beauty of the ferry business is, you get to be on the boat in the daytime and you get to be home at night." Albright lives in New Jersey and drives about forty minutes to get to the boat in Highlands, New Jersey. Arriving there at 5:15 A.M., he and his three fellow crewmen shape up the vessel. They start loading people at five forty-five, and with Albright handling the ropes, or in seafaring parlance, the "lines," the boat leaves the dock at six-fifteen. Most of the passengers work for firms in the financial district of Manhattan, and they pay $28 for the round-trip. Some sit and read the papers; others stand on deck and catch the breeze. There is a bar on board, which is busier in the afternoon than in the morning, and it has a full-time bartender, although Albright sometimes helps out serving drinks.

The eighty-three-foot, high-speed catamaran cruises the waters of the Narrows and New York Harbor at thirty knots, or about thirty-five miles an hour, making the trip to Manhattan in forty minutes. Upon reaching the Wall Street area, where again Albright handles the lines, passengers disembark; but the crew must do its job quickly so they can return to New Jersey and pick up a second morning load of passengers bound for Wall Street.

Forty minutes later, back at Wall Street, Albright helps these commuters off the boat and braces himself for a long day of waiting at Pier 11. The monotony is broken only when a group of tourists hires the boat for a sightseeing run. But the revenues from the trip, which could be several

hundred dollars, go only to the owner of the ferry, a company called Seastreak. The crew does not get paid for the extra work. Many deckhands with other companies are members of the Seafarers Union, but Albright and his mates on the *Express II* are not. Sightseeing tour or no, the crew must be back before 5:30 P.M. to pick up passengers for the evening run to Highlands. There in New Jersey, after cleaning up and doing some paperwork, the crew is ready at about seven o'clock to call it quits for the day. Because they put in almost fourteen hours straight, they work only four days a week. Albright says deckhands make $30,000 a year and up, "depending on how long you've been here." The Seastreak company operates three ferries, all of them based in New Jersey.

Raised on Long Island, Albright grew up with boats, and decided early on that he wanted to make his living on the water. He attended New York Maritime College and, before getting into urban transportation, captained private yachts and worked as a third mate on oil tankers.

IX. THE ARTISTS

78. PIANO MAN

Salary: $15,000 in a bad year, $35,000 in a good one

Hours: Approximately 35 a week, 5 days a week

Benefits: No

Union: Yes

Experience or Requirements: Played bars, clubs, and hotels from California to New York

Use computer: No

Workplace: Restaurants, hotels, bars

Risks: One's ego

When people pass the McDonald's restaurant near Wall Street and see him at the piano, there are a million places Gordon McLee would rather be. "It's an embarrassing job to have, because you sit near the window and almost everyone looks and laughs and points," says McLee, who plays everything from old Motown hits to classical music. McLee imagines the gawkers looking into the fast-food place saying, "I guess he really needs a job," and he wants to tell them that, yes, that may be true, but he's done fancier joints from here to California. "I feel like I want to hand out a flyer that says, 'Here are the other places I've played.'"

In his more sanguine moments, McLee concedes the passersby are simply fascinated by the sight of a piano player at Mickey D's. But those moments are fleeting. "The only thing that makes it palatable," he says, "is that it's a shiny black grand piano, so you know you're playing an instrument that looks classy." McLee has been at pianos since he was six years old, when his parents bought him a Schumann upright. He especially loves old popular standards and show tunes. He believes in the ancient dictum, "not much but well." "Guys claim they know thousands of songs. I don't think there are that many good songs in the universe. I don't think I know more than 500 songs, maybe 700. That's about thirty to forty hours of music."

McLee was born in Rockford, Illinois, but moved to Los Angeles, where he played at the Comedy Store on Sunset Boulevard. Then in 1981 he came to the city of his dreams, New York. Besides McDonald's, he entertains part-time at three other locations around town — the Hotel Intercontinental, Frankie and Johnny's steakhouse, and Parnell's. At those places, he sometimes plays his own compositions, and he can tell when he's connecting with the audience. "You focus on a table or two of people who are listening to you and enjoying you, and the next thing you know an hour's gone by. They're connected to you. That's what makes it so difficult at McDonald's. You feel like no one's listening to you."

Work for musicians is very insecure, so he takes what he can get—twenty-four hours a week at McDonald's and another ten or so at nightspots around Manhattan. "Most owners are not friendly people. They're beautiful to their customers, but not too kind to their employees," he says. Frequently the experiences are humiliating. Once, he was playing at a popular restaurant in Manhattan when "the manager comes in, and he decides that my hair isn't combed properly. And I'm sitting there at the piano ten minutes before I'm supposed to start. He actually escorted me to the men's room. He told the girl who books special events that I'm not good-looking enough for 'A-class events.'"

One of the more pleasant times of McLee's day is riding the ferry between Staten Island, where he lives, and his jobs in Manhattan. On one trip he had the good fortune to meet a guy who became his agent and who receives a cut of his earnings. McLee opined that if he had finished college or acquired some other skill, he would be more financially secure and maybe even have health insurance. His union, the American Federation of Musicians, Local 802, offers a plan for about $1,300 a year, "But I can't afford it." Then again, when asked if there is anything else he'd enjoy more than playing music, he hesitates for a moment and says, "I've always thought about that. I guess not."

79. STREET PHOTOGRAPHER

Salary: At least $20,000 a year

Hours: 12 a day, 7 days a week

Benefits: None

Union: No

Experience or Requirements: Years of shooting

Use computer: No

Workplace: Staten Island Ferry, Coney Island, tourist spots

Risks: Uninformed police officers

Happy people like to be photographed. On that theory, Louis R. Mendes travels around the city looking for families and friends who want their good times recorded for posterity. He carries two cameras, and he specializes in taking double exposures, which superimpose images on each other: a mother and a child, a girlfriend and a boyfriend, a family and the moon. "In the last ten years I've gone through eighty-five Polaroid Spectra cameras," says Mendes, who is fifty-nine years old and has been in this line of work for close to three decades. "When you think Polaroid, you think 'Oh, I can do that.' Everyone thinks of Polaroid as cheap, but when they see my results, they know differently."

Mendes estimates there are several dozen others in New York City doing what he does full-time. He charges $20 for a double exposure and $10 for a simple picture. From his home in Harlem, he takes public transportation to places where people are out having fun, and he often does some old-fashioned fair barking.

"Get it while you're young! In twenty years it'll be a classic!" "You ought to be in pictures!"

Sometimes people are drawn to him by the sight of the 1940s accordion-lens Speed Graphic he carries on a shoulder strap. It is a relic that distinguishes him from other street photographers who rely only on a Polaroid. Up until a few years ago, Mendes was hassled frequently by police, who would ticket him or even arrest him for peddling without a license. Now he carries in his shoulder bag a copy of a U.S. Court of Appeals decision declaring photography protected under the First Amendment. Police still stop and question him, but he hasn't been arrested in three years.

During the Christmas season Mendes strolls around Rockefeller Center. In the summer he likes to go to Coney Island. If the weather is bad, he'll ride the Staten Island Ferry. Sometimes he stands outside the Municipal Building in Manhattan, waiting for just-married couples to emerge. Ever on the lookout for prospects, he gathers pamphlets announcing block parties, dances, and other events and he notes the dates. From time to time, he travels. In 1995, he went to Washington, D.C., for the Million Man March and made $2,100 in one day.

Back in the 1960s Mendes had a job in the strobe repair department at Honeywell. But by 1970 he decided, "When you work for a company, they dictate what you do." And so, in his spare time, he began indulging what up to then had been a hobby, going around town and taking pictures of people. He now makes what he considers to be, for him, a decent living, and he's convinced himself that a health policy is not necessary. "If you're healthy you don't need insurance....I find that most people who work in the street are healthier than people that work in an office." Unlike studio photographers, Mendes has to work quickly. "You have to work with people, and all I have is a couple of minutes [to] bring out the best that I can find in them." And unlike many photojournalists, he's always looking for scenes that are happy. "I don't like the blood and guts. I like shooting love stories."

80. TATTOO ARTIST

Salary: More than $60,000 a year
Hours: Sometimes all night
Benefits: None
Union: No

Experience or Requirements: An apprenticeship, certification from Department of Health, associate's degree in art
Use computer: No
Workplace: A chair
Risks: Cuts and burns

For years, he had to do his thing underground. Then in 1997 New York City legalized tattooing for those with some training in the craft. And thirty-five-year-old Sean Vasquez has never been busier. He has worked for as long as thirteen hours straight, without even going to the bathroom. He holds his tattoo machine carefully, his face close to the skin, gaze fixed with intensity, as he burns symbols, pictures, and words into the flesh of clients. People don't go to Vasquez to get "Mom" stamped on their biceps. His work is often something this side of Picasso's "Guernica"; occasionally, it's as blunt as a rendering of Christ or a smoking gun. Customers pay several hundred dollars or more, depending on the complexity of the design.

Hours after the sun goes down, Vasquez is found tattooing twenty-seven-year-old Steve Mills. Mills sits silently, his left arm resting on a paper towel, as Vasquez does his work. Mills says he is relying on Vasquez to use intuition and professional judgment in putting on the tattoos. Vasquez is getting strong vibrations. "I kind of got an idea of his personality and what his views were," he says. "The only thing I [saw] was pro-God, antigovernment. It's got to be covert, kind of subtle....Putting in the outline, the beginning of the design...from here I'll develop it." Already, Mills has on his body little skulls juxtaposed with bigger skulls. There are also teardrops. Some of the more intricate designs take up to forty hours, over the course of a week or more, of sitting at the mercy of the iron, he says. "Compared with a lot of people, I'm just starting up," says Mills, who has been adding images one at a time over eight years. "It hurts but it's worth it." He describes the process as like "getting a piece of steel shoved into your muscle tissue."

Vasquez doesn't like to talk much when he's tattooing. He had previously worked for himself but now is employed by Kaleidoscope Tattooing (which has since changed its name to Sacred Tattoo). The setting is a loft on Houston Street, located between Soho, with its art galleries and boutiques, and Little Italy. Across the street, a video store advertises Triple-X-rated films. "Hindu deities are one of the things I like to do," says Vasquez, in a burst of verbosity. "I'm not religious but I like doing them. They represent the opener of doorways. It's also good luck. It kind of brings you the things you're looking for." Vasquez received an associate's degree in art from Kingsborough Community College in Brooklyn. He traveled the world, picking up tattooing along the way. Wes Wood, who owns Sacred Tattoo and also operates a tattoo supply company called Unimax, says there are about 150 tattoo artists in the city, and many of them make about $500 a week. Only the veterans with ten years of experience are making what Vasquez makes, he says.

The craft of tattooing can be learned in a day, Wood says, but it takes years to learn the *art* of tattooing. By law, tattoo artists must take a course in sterilization. Vasquez, who does about twenty clients a week, takes a cab to and from his residence in the nearby Lower East Side of Manhattan. He says his job is stressful, but he finds a certain peace in it. "I solve a lot of my issues when I'm tattooing. It's not a very aggressive act. It's a very mellow act."

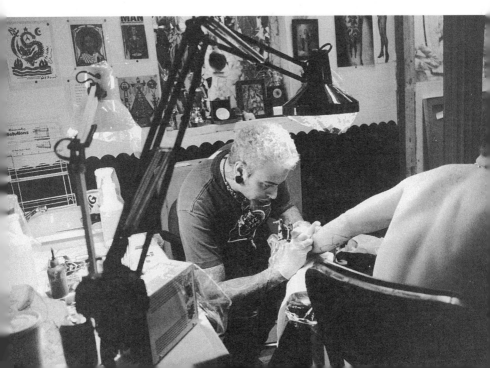

81. VISUAL ARTIST

Income: $30,000 to $50,000, minus expenses
Hours: 18 to 20 a day, sometimes 7 days a week
Benefits: None
Union: No
Experience or Requirements: Bachelor's degrees in art and in education
Use computer: Yes
Workplace: A studio
Risks: Hazardous chemicals

Brett Cook-Dizney keeps a hand-printed sign on the front door of his 4,000-square-foot studio. The words serve as his constant reminder and motivation: "Leave your painting for one day and your painting will leave you for three." So Cook-Dizney often toils days and nights on a couple of hours' sleep, doing the research for and creating the art that is the passion of his life. The pieces for which he is best known are multimedia works, done on plywood and depicting everyday people in urban America. They often include writings by the subjects of the paintings, and sometimes even photographs. "It's about telling these people's lives in different ways," says Cook-Dizney, age thirty. He just finished a stint as artist-in-residence at the Studio Museum in Harlem, for which he was paid a stipend. And he just recently sold one of his works for $5,000. But to pay the bills and eat, he has to earn money in a variety of other ways. He also is often at his laptop computer pounding out ideas for grants. And four days a week he's at the Satellite Academy, an alternative high school on the Lower East Side of Manhattan, where he teaches history and other courses, incorporating visual art in the lessons. Approximately half of his annual income goes toward the rent of his huge studio in Harlem. He lives farther downtown in Chelsea and commutes by subway.

Cook-Dizney is a self-described dreamer. His dream is to capture, in his art, people from communities across America, especially urban communities, and then to give the art back to the people. Literally. Cook-Dizney has placed hundreds of his art pieces on buildings around New York and other cities. Often the buildings are abandoned, but sometimes they are not. He never asks permission of the owner, and he knows full well that some people will take and keep pieces for themselves. As he speaks, he is preparing to travel to San Diego, where the plan is first to interview residents of three communities very different from each other in ethnicity and average income. He will then do eight large paintings, and place them on buildings in those neighborhoods. "They will be about geographical and class and racial separation," he says of the planned pieces. "They could live a long time, or they could disappear." His expenses for the two-week project are being paid by the University of California at San Diego.

Having had his works displayed at several galleries recently, including Exit Art on Broadway in Soho and the Studio Museum in Harlem, Cook-Dizney is beginning to have a sense of himself as an established artist. "It's almost ten years now since I've really thought of myself as this professional."

Often he uses spray paint for his pieces, although he knows it is not the best thing for his health. "As I've gotten older, I've gotten better at being responsible about the hazards of my job," he says, pointing out that, for one thing, he has fans in the studio. The spray paint is certainly hazardous, he says "but I think many art practices are. And I think that there's a certain compromise that artists make by putting themselves around materials." His work and his life are one. "I always have my sketchbook, everywhere I go, all the time," he says, "and pretty much my whole life is orchestrated to my work." He adds: "I think people often say that about my work, that it looks very joyful. And for me, when I paint, it's a lark. I play music really loud. I dance. I sing....It's something I like to do."

X. THE
FRINGE-DWELLERS

82. SQUEEGEE MAN

Salary: A few hundred up to perhaps a couple of thousand dollars a year

Hours: 5 a day, mornings and evenings, sometimes less, sometimes more

Benefits: None

Union: No

Experience or Requirements: None

Use computer: No

Workplace: A street corner

Risks: Arrests

Holding in his left hand one of his tools—a dirty rag—Levine Bradley feels like the last of a dying breed of workers. The person who's been pushing him out of business is Mayor Rudolph Giuliani, who through his police department has effectively made it a crime to be a squeegee man. Bradley, age thirty-nine, doesn't carry a squeegee anymore. Police are primed to bust anyone with one of those window-washing devices in hand, especially an unkempt, homeless-looking black man. Instead, Bradley is carrying a gray-colored rag that he can tuck into his back pocket at a moment's notice. A bottle containing alcohol and water for moistening the rag sits nearby.

On nice warm days, Bradley and his fellow squeegee man Larry like to spend as many hours as they can washing windows—or trying to. Sometimes a driver will curse at them the moment they put their rag on the windshield. Some get so angry it seems that they want to fight. Larry says that in the past he could sometimes make $100 in a day. But things are a little riskier now; these days, he's lucky to make $50, and Bradley says he's been arrested twenty times in the past year. Cops pull him in on disorderly conduct and harassment charges when they catch him trying to wash car windows. The arrests don't bother him too much, he says, because the judges generally lets him go the day after the arrest.

Bradley explains how he became a squeegee man: "I lost my job doing construction about three years ago, and I never got another job. I seen my cousin doing this and I seen it ain't hurting nobody. I'd rather do this than rob somebody. I don't want to put a gun in my hand no more. I'd rather use a squeegee or a rag. The cops said if we walk across the street with a squeegee in our hands they be locking us up, so no carrying squeegees.... I don't do this for drugs. I do it to get something to eat, to have money in

my pocket." A tenth-grade dropout from the Bronx, Bradley has been living with a friend and recently has started to divide his working time between washing car windows and selling daily newspapers that a friend provides him. Bradley says he has several friends who help him out in ways he can't fully disclose. "I got so many people who come and say, 'Here, take this. I know you're trying to do the right thing.'"

Larry, who doesn't want his full name used because he doesn't want to "shame" his family, especially his children, with whom he does not live, complains about the city's get-tough policy on squeegee men. "Giuliani made a law that we can't wash windows. I don't know why. The majority of us, we're really decent. It's just that we had a bad time." In his case, it was crack that "really fucked me up," Larry says. "I'm embarrassed by what I do....Some people curse you out, shout, 'Get off my car.' But you ain't gonna get out of no car on me, you know. I ain't gonna let nobody hurt me," he says. "We're out here trying to live any way we can."

83. HOMELESS BOTTLE-COLLECTOR

Salary: Several thousand dollars a year	**Use computer:** No
Hours: All day	**Environment:** The streets of Manhattan
Benefits: None	**Risks:** Arrests for various infractions
Union: No	of the law, sickness from exposure
Experience or Requirements: None	and alcohol

"I picked up two hundred and forty cans today and I bought this," thirty-eight-year-old Milledge James says as he sits at the curb on Broadway, just across the street from City Hall. He holds up the brand-new Walkman radio he purchased earlier in the day for $12. He has been sitting peacefully, the headset covering his ears, listening to soft pop music on 106.7 LITE-FM. Beside him, to his right, is a thirty-gallon bag with yet another 60 empty soda cans that he says are worth $3. "This pays for my food, my beer, whatever." This day, like others so far in the week, is sunny. And that means good pickings for James. "Whenever it's hot, it's more money because everybody drinks sodas." It's not only bottles and cans that he looks for, but also empty Marlboro cigarette packs, which contain coupons worth five cents toward the purchase of another pack. "So that helps me out too," he says.

He keeps his earnings in his socks. In more than a decade of earning his cash this way, he has never been held up. A thin man with hollow eyes and a strong stutter, James has been living on the streets pretty steadily since 1982, when he quit his job packing groceries at a Gristede's supermarket. He was angry at the managers because they kept sending him on deliveries that didn't yield much in the way of tips, but now in a twist of fate he relies on supermarkets to pay him for the bottles he takes to them daily. Last year, "I busted a store window 'cause they wouldn't take my cans." That was at a supermarket at Seventieth Street and Amsterdam Avenue, he says. After his act of vandalism, he simply sat and waited for the cops to come and take him. A judge sentenced him to six months on Rikers Island, and he served three months of the sentence. James has been arrested a total of about twenty times, mostly for jumping turnstiles.

Occasionally, when he wants to take a bath or when he is simply too weary of the streets, he stays at a homeless shelter. His fundamental problem, he acknowledges, is alcohol. The week before this interview, he was on a binge so devastating he ended up at city-run Bellevue Hospital. When he stays at a homeless shelter, he usually is served a light breakfast the morning after, and he receives money for subway fare. Then he's on the streets again, for weeks or months. "I was sick. I mean I was drunk," he says, referring to the recent binge that landed him at Bellevue. But it wasn't so bad an experience that it relieved him of his love for beer. "That's what I'm gonna do with this money, when I cash it," he says. "But I'm not gonna get drunk."

James was born in Harlem and attended Martin Luther King High School until the age of nineteen, when he dropped out. He was abusing drugs at the time. Leaving behind a stable working-class family that included five sisters and two brothers, all Jehovah's Witnesses, he commenced life on the street, and he has not seen his family since the late 1970s. He will go look for them "someday when I get a regular job," which he hopes is not too far in the future. "Right now I'm tired of being homeless," he says.

84. WELFARE-TO-WORK WORKER

Salary: $8,840 a year
Hours: 7 a day, 3 days a week
Benefits: Medicaid
Union: No

Experience or Requirements: Need and elegibility for public assistance
Use computer: No
Workplace: A park
Risks: Job assignments potentially injurious to health

With her asthma, which flares up periodically, the last place Cathy Ramsey wanted to work is around vegetation. Now here she was, picking up and bagging garbage in one of the most grassy, tree-filled parts of the city—Prospect Park. But thirty-nine-year-old Ramsey does not believe in confrontation. She never asked her doctor to send a letter excusing her from the park assignment. "My doctor doesn't know I'm here, and if he did, it wouldn't matter, because when welfare tells you to go somewhere, that's where you got to go," said Ramsey.

Ramsey and her seven children—five of whom are asthmatic—were receiving $340 every week through the federal assistance program called Aid to Families with Dependent Children. But in fulfillment of pledges by politicians to end "welfare as we know it," officials told her she had to work for her government check. And so she was put on the city's Work Experience Program. Assigned to park duty, she was found one summer day wearing her green cap, stabbing leaves and empty cups and other refuse with a nail-tipped stick. It was a far cry from the office work for which she had been preparing at Monroe College in the Bronx. "Even when it's raining, you're out here bagging and stacking...and you have to bring your own raincoat."

Contacted months after she was interviewed in the park, Ramsey has-gotten a job in the private sector, as a night security guard at a senior citizens home. She is making just under $7 an hour, not much above minimum wage, and what's more, because she has a full-time job, she is told by

welfare officials that she is no longer eligible for Medicaid—even though her new job offers no health coverage for her or her children. She is happy about the job but acknowledges that, yes, "in a way," it is a mixed blessing. One morning, hours before her tour as a security guard begins, she is preparing to take two of her children to the doctor; they are suffering with fevers. She says she will have to pay out of her pocket for whatever medications they require. She will feel the pinch. Already she is trying to scrimp because of the cost of antibiotics she had recently purchased for herself. Although suffering financially, she ultimately prefers the security guard position to the work in the park, and says she is confident that she and her children will someday have a better life. "I've got God on my side," she says.

85. STREET CLEANER

Salary: $9,980 a year	**Experience or Requirements:** None
Hours: 6 a day, 5 days a week	**Use computer:** No
Benefits: Vacation	**Workplace:** The sidewalks and curbs
Union: No	of the West Side
	Risks: Relapse to life of drug abuse

The bus comes every weekday morning at seven-thirty to pick up Richard Adams and the others. It takes them downtown to Eighty-Second Street and Broadway, where they get their equipment (a broom, a dustpan, and a huge trash bin) and start their workday. On this sunny afternoon, Adams has just swept up a pan full of dirt, wrappings, and other litter from the curb at Broadway just south of Ninety-Sixth Street. He dumps the trash into the blue bin with wheels that he pulls with him along the fourteen-block stretch of Broadway that is his territory. He wears a uniform of blue pants, blue cap, blue T-shirt (with an American flag on the left sleeve), black shoes, and gloves. His equipment bears insignias indicating he works with the Doe Fund and that his motto is "ready, willing and able."

Adams, age forty-one, was recently strung out on crack and living in homeless shelters. While he was recovering at Bellevue Hospital, counselors there put him in touch with the business-sponsored, nonprofit Doe Fund, which is dedicated to helping hard-core cases such as Adams find a niche in the world of work. According to Adams, the raison d'être and driving philosophy of the program is "they don't want you to be on public assistance." And so they put him on a rigid schedule and a tight budget, and Adams sweeps and dumps for six hours a day, with two fifteen-minute breaks. One break is at 10:00 A.M., the other at 2:00 P.M., and there is half an hour off for lunch, beginning at noon. The idea is for him to stay with the job for a year and, at the same time, continue his drug counseling program, learn a skill, and have some money.

Along with others in the program, Adams is staying at a facility operated by the Doe Fund on Frederick Douglass Boulevard and 155th Street

up in Harlem–Washington Heights. Out of his weekly paycheck, the Fund automatically deducts $30, which he is required to keep as savings, as well as $65 for his bed. He gets three sick and five personal days, plus a week off with pay, and he has health coverage, not through the job, but through the government's Medicaid program.

Adams is just several days from beginning a high school equivalency course, which he plans to attend during his off-hours. He expects to save a total of $1,020 by the end of his year with the program and at that point he should be close to obtaining a job outside the Doe Fund. "At that stage of savings, you should be at a stage of employment," he says, relating the expectations of the Doe Fund. He hopes one day to find employment working in some capacity with computers.

86. CAR WASHER

Salary: $18,000 to $21,000 a year

Hours: 12 a day, sometimes 7 days a week

Benefits: None

Union: No

Experience or Requirements: None

Use computer: No

Workplace: Car wash

Risks: Exhaust fumes

The days are long, and often the tips are very short, but forty-eight-year-old Jean Diomele shows no lack of energy. Eyes flashing, mouth bellowing orders, he sometimes seems to be going on automatic, just like the machines at the car wash. As a manager of Suzie's Automated Hand Car Wash, Diomele supervises and works with a team of immigrants who dry vehicles that have just exited the gauntlet of automated sprayers and flopping, soapy rags. "Hey, yo, the customer is waiting," Diomele yells to a dryer who is a bit slow in getting to a car that has just finished the washing process.

At one point, Diomele grabs a rag in seeming disgust from one of the employees and completes the job himself. Employees appear on occasion to be muttering at him in their native languages, which span a range of tongues: Spanish, French, and Haitian Creole. Diomele can answer each of them in kind. "Mi papá es dominicano, mi mamá es haitiana. ¿Tu sabes?" ("My mother is from the Dominican Republic, my father is Haitian. You know?")

As the chief of the crew of dryers, who include young men from Mexico, Ecuador, Haiti, El Salvador, Honduras, and Mali, he earns a relatively respectable salary, he says, "I can make $450 or more, with tips, if it's a busy week." Tips go into a two-foot-long miniature blue-and-white car with a slit in the top. About ten fistfuls of dollars can be seen through the transparent top of the little vehicle. The men share the tips at the end of the day. Workers get paid a base salary according to the boss's judgment of their dependability. If they hustle and are willing to work all day for seven days a week, the dryers under Diomele's supervision make perhaps $300 or more, including tips.

Like those he oversees, Diomele sometimes puts in seven-day weeks. "I work a seven-day week when I need money." He did similar work in the

Bronx for twelve years before switching a year ago to his current job, located on Atlantic Avenue near Vanderbilt Avenue in Brooklyn. Diomele has eight children living in two households, both of which he supports financially. One is in Washington Heights, where he lives with his current wife and five children, and the other is back in the Dominican Republic, where his former wife lives with his other children. He has a driver's license but prefers car washing to driving a taxi, the chosen line of work for many immigrants of his background. He knows one thing, he says, speaking brusquely as he goes from task to task, drying cars, putting rags in the washing machine, and shouting out orders to younger men who seem to mostly ignore him: "I can't sell drugs."

87. FORMER PROSTITUTE

Salary: $39,000 to $52,000 a year	**Experience or Requirements:** None
Hours: Nights	**Use computer:** No
Benefits: None	**Workplace:** Dark streets
Union: No	**Risks:** Diseases, violence

Kai H. worked "the stroll" for seventeen years, on the streets of the South Bronx, in Newark, New Jersey, and wherever else she could find guys willing to pay for oral sex. She actually liked the work, or so she convinced herself, and the money wasn't bad. "A good day could be anywhere from $150 to $300," she says. Sometimes she'd meet a gentle fellow who would be her steady for a while. One man, whom she described as involved in organized crime, even took her with him overseas. "I've been to London, England. I've flown on a Concorde," she says. Asked how she met the man who took her across the Atlantic, the thirty-seven-year-old Kai recalls: "I was standing on the corner. He was cute, he had money, and I sucked good." When they went to London together, "I stayed in the hotel. That's all I was allowed to do."

Having decided in the past year to change her life, she has been working as a volunteer with a group called From Our Streets With Dignity (FROST'D), which counsels streetwalkers and gives out condoms. She has applied for welfare, but she doesn't like the city's policy of sending applicants out to work cleaning up parks or sweeping the streets. "I ain't going around the street picking up nobody's garbage," she says. No, she says, she will find something helping people or working in an office. "I feel experience is the best teacher, and I'm experienced."

As a prostitute, Kai found that the streets brought her money but were otherwise not friendly. She estimates that she was arrested maybe 200 times, generally for "loitering for the purpose of prostitution." And because she didn't use a pimp and therefore had no one to protect her, Kai was an easy mark for predators, and, she says, she has been raped about five times. Once while she was in a weed-filled lot with a man, about to perform oral sex, he suddenly pulled a knife and slashed her on the left side of her neck, drawing blood. She ran away and found a friend who gave her some heroin, which eased the pain. The dope also made it easier for her to put a scarf around her neck and go right back out on the streets, looking for customers.

Drugs, first heroin and then crack, were always a part of her life on the stroll. But she never shot them into her veins, she says. As for concerns about HIV, she has taken the test a number of times in the previous year and was negative each time. Her lowest point was when she was living in huts in little shanty communities in the Bronx. Guilt overwhelmed her as she realized she was neglecting her two sons, who were growing up in Brooklyn with her mother. One of them is the offspring of a trick. It was one of the few times she had vaginal sex with a customer. "He was white," says Kai. "And it was the only time a condom ever broke on me." Kai doesn't want her last name used because she believes her sons might be harassed at school if students know their mother was a prostitute.

88. FORMER DRUG DEALER

Salary: Up to $100,000 a year	**Experience or Requirements:** Nerve
Hours: Mostly evenings and nights	and recklessness
Benefits: None	**Use computer:** No
Union: No	**Workplace:** Outdoors/indoors
	Risks: Jail, murder

There were parties every weekend, and in his spare time he hung out on the corner with the guys. His car was a recent model BMW, and the money was coming in at a rate of several thousand dollars a week. Not bad for a high-school dropout. But as with many professions that yield high returns, there was a psychic price that Carlos Medina (not his real last name) had to pay. Like looking over his shoulder, wondering if he might run into those guys he had stuck up the week before. Or whether some dope fiend who didn't like the crack Medina had sold him might come back with vengeance on his mind.

Medina's life in the fast lane began roughly in 1986, when he left John F. Kennedy High School in the Bronx. He started off by selling crack. He'd get 100 bottles, pay his supplier $6 for each one, and then put the contents into smaller bottles that he would sell for profits of $500 a day or more. "When I was really selling I was making more than five grand a week. I would get my share and it would be a couple of thousand." On a whim he bought a stolen BMW for $4,500 in cash and drugs. A good typist, he contracted with counterfeiters who provided him false Social Security cards, so he could fill them out and sell them to illegal aliens, sometimes at $200 or more a pop, depending on how desperate the immigrant was. "I would spend as much as I was making: partying, women, cars, going back and forth to the island," he said, referring to his native Dominican Republic. Medina said he used to carry a gun and would do target practice in a basement. "It would make a hole this big," he says, cupping his hands. He lived this life until one day in 1995.

That was when he finally got busted during a delivery of drugs, and police discovered he was armed with a pistol. "I pled guilty to possession of fifteen grams of coke and a gun, a .357 revolver," he says. Medina served time in jail and was released just months before this interview. He is now thirty years old and earns up to $575 a week from two jobs. At his main job, in the Bronx, not far from his upper Manhattan residence, he helps to create an online newsletter for a group of lawyers. For that, he earns $400 but no other benefits. His part-time job is to teach word processing to private clients. For a total of about twelve hours of teaching each week, he earns between $140 and $175. Mentally, every day, he struggles to break with his recent past. "From my group of friends, we were twenty-two. Out of all of them eight are dead, five are in jail, two are junkies and the rest are married or have businesses." Medina hopes to end up in the last group.

XI. THE EDUCATORS

89. "SPECIAL ED" TEACHER

Salary: $35,400 a year
Hours: 8:30 A.M. to 2:30 P.M.,
Monday through Friday
Benefits: Health, pension, vacation
Union: Yes

Experience or Requirements: College degree
in education or related field
Use computer: Yes
Workplace: A classroom
Risks: Frustration and discouragement

Teaching a special education class is rough. It can wound the ego of even the most confident teacher, like Amarilis Lantigua. Special education is the euphemistic term given to classes for children who have learning or behavioral problems. Critics have long complained that the classes are dumping grounds for minority boys. "Most people find special education the roughest because we have to deal with not only learning disabilities but behavioral problems and it's very frustrating," says Lantigua, age thirty-four, who teaches sixth grade at Woodside Intermediate School in Queens. She has the added responsibility of being a bilingual teacher. Her fifteen or so students are from Spanish-speaking countries such as Mexico, Colombia, the Dominican Republic, and Peru. Sometimes she finds the challenges daunting. "You spend a while working with them and you end up at square one. Sometimes you feel like, Am I teaching? Are they learning? Because you look and you don't see much progress."

She recalls one student in particular. He took things from other children and was often disruptive in class. Lantigua worked with the boy one on one and tried to give him easier homework, but he would never do it. Finally, she called in his parents and attempted to convince them that he needed long-term help from a therapist. The family rejected the idea, saying they had tried therapy once for a couple of months, and that the boy was "just like one of his uncles" and there was nothing more to expect from him. In losing that battle, Lantigua was bloodied but unbowed. She finds on occasion that she has to massage her ego. "I'm the best they have," says the Dominican-born Lantigua, "so that gives me the strength to keep going. I know that it could have been worse for them, without me."

Lantigua is at school from eight-thirty in the morning until two-thirty in the afternoon, but on average she puts in another hour and a half preparing for classes. She lives in Queens and drives to and from the school. Often she's up late at night at home putting together materials that she will use the next day. "Especially with special ed, we have to prepare a whole lot more…they're slower. We cannot just write a lesson on the board. We have to accommodate, use special strategies, charts. We have to draw pictures that help explain what we would normally just write. And where do I do all this? Home." Lantigua acknowledges that she gets especially anxious when supervisors come, as they periodically do, to observe her class. "You could be teaching for twenty years and you will see that that still causes stress," she says. Lantigua, a teacher for four years, has a master's degree in bilingual education and hopes to start work on her doctorate within a year. She spent several years in the Air Force before becoming first a classroom paraprofessional and then a full-fledged teacher, as well as a member of the politically powerful United Federation of Teachers.

Although many teachers use their summer recess to travel or relax, Lantigua teaches summer classes, adding up to several thousand dollars to her regular $35,400-a-year salary. Lantigua is not sure she will be able to teach the rest of her working life. "Sometimes I'm drained," she says. "Everything gets to be tiresome. Right now I have the energy. But the day I don't feel capable, that I don't have the energy, I won't do it."

90. ADJUNCT PROFESSOR

Salary: About $24,000 a year
Hours: Frequently 12 a day
Benefits: Health, when teaching at least six credits
Union: Yes

Experience or Requirements: Bachelor's degree, advanced degrees
Use computer: Yes
Workplace: Classrooms
Risks: Wounded ego, propertyless old age

She has two master's degrees and four decades of work experience. But for an adjunct professor of college English, the pay is poor and the grind is unceasing. In her most recent semester of teaching, sixty-three-year-old Marcia Newfield shuttled back and forth between two colleges, one in Manhattan, the Borough of Manhattan Community College (BMCC) and the other in Brooklyn, Long Island University (LIU), where she had heavy teaching loads. On the side, she supplemented her income as a "literary midwife," helping others write and edit their manuscripts, and over the years, she has written poetry and children's books. But she's embarrassed at her annual income, which is almost always under $30,000. Like hundreds of other underpaid and overworked adjunct professors in the city and country, Newfield has no job protection and no pension. She says she sometimes feels hurt and ashamed that in her early sixties she has virtually nothing she can call her own.

Through committees and unions at the colleges where she has been teaching, Newfield has been trying to fight for improved conditions for adjuncts. So far, the victories have been negligible. Describing her schedule the previous semester, she says: "I would leave here at nine (in the morning) to get to LIU at ten. I'd teach from ten to twelve at LIU, and then I'd go to BMCC and teach from four-fifteen to eight-thirty." She prepared for classes on subway rides. Because each class was a different course—and because the students were at vastly different levels—she had to do separate "preps," or preparations, for them. College adjuncts, even the young ones, often look and feel exhausted. "My biggest task was to remember which day it was," says Newfield, who lives on Manhattan's Upper West Side.

In her worst moments, Newfield gets quite depressed and believes this is the way things will be until she dies—hustling between colleges, struggling to teach writing and literature to scores of young New Yorkers, many of them immigrants, at a salary half that of a librarian. Social Security and a couple of modest Individual Retirement Accounts (IRAs) will be her salvation if she has to retire.

The upside of her career, Newfield says with some delight, is that she is able to have her summers mostly free to write and to paint. Many adjuncts teach in the summer but Newfield chooses not to. And in the end, she feels that she has been living her life according to deeply held principles, that life is about growth and appreciation of beautiful things. "When you work from nine-to-five for fifty weeks a year," she says, "it's very hard to keep up your art habit....I write about art for a magazine called ART, and I'm going away to Bread and Puppet Theater for a week." In and out of the classroom, she fights within herself a battle over those very principles. "It's very hard to maintain self-esteem in this culture if you're not rich and you have gone with your values."

91. UPPER SCHOOL DIRECTOR

Salary: $90,000 a year, plus another several thousand paid into an investment plan
Hours: About 55 a week, Monday through Friday
Benefits: Health, retirement, investment fund (TIAA-CREF), vacation
Union: No

Experience or Requirements: Bachelor's degree, two master's degrees, jobs at other private schools
Use computer: Yes
Workplace: Office, classroom, hallways, gymnasium
Risks: None reported

As an educator, forty-one-year-old Christopher Teare is in an enviable position. He's the director of the upper school—grades nine through twelve—at Berkeley-Carroll in Brooklyn, and every time a teaching spot opens up, the résumés come pouring in. "We get hundreds of applications for every job," he says. He goes through the mounds of applications and winnows them down to a few, preferring graduates of prestigious colleges.

Prospective teachers choose Berkeley-Carroll for the same reason parents do. Parents pay $14,000 a year expecting the school to be relatively free of discipline problems, and it is the job of the director to keep it that way. Earlier in the day, Teare had met with other administrators about a boy suspected of making prank calls to a classmate. They listened to a recording of the call, agreed the young man was guilty, and debated what his punishment should be. The possibilities, says Teare, range from suspension to expulsion. Teare has had to expel students for plagiarism and even for theft, but acts of aggression are rare.

While private school teachers get paid less than their public school counterparts, Teare earns considerably more than his counterparts. He gets $90,000 a year, about $10,000 more than a public high school principal. Besides performing administrative duties—like presiding over meetings, going over budgets, and arranging for guest speakers—he teaches a course or two every semester, in literature or vocabulary. Students stream in and out of his office, to confer about an assignment or a problem. He usually arrives at the school at about seven-thirty in the morning, walking from his nearby home in the Park Slope section, and he often doesn't get home until nine o'clock at night, especially when there are important athletic events or parents' meetings he must attend. Teare got his bachelor's degree from Amherst, and holds master's degrees from the Columbia University Graduate School of Journalism and St. John's College in Annapolis, Maryland.

Neither teachers nor administrators at Berkeley-Carroll are union members, which pleases Teare. He believes private schools function well because they don't have to deal with unions or layers of bureaucracy. Nonetheless, when it comes to the city's best public high schools, where entrance is by examination, some Berkeley-Carroll parents are thinking of jumping ship. Teare tries to convince them to stay. "I'll soon be talking with parents of an eighth-grader who has a chance of getting into Stuyvesant, and they will have to make a decision." He is referring to Peter Stuyvesant High School in Manhattan, nationally recognized for its science and other programs. Teare's pitch to the parents is that Stuyvesant cannot offer the small classes (as few as five pupils) or personal attention that students get at Berkeley-Carroll.

Private schools are by definition exclusive, but Teare says he and his boss, the headmistress of Berkeley-Carroll, try to make the upper school ethnically diverse. About a third of the 200 students are minority, a number of them receiving financial assistance. As upper school director, Teare works through most of the summer but takes a month off between late July and August. After six years at Berkeley-Carroll, he is planning to move at the end of the semester to South Hamilton, Massachusetts, where he will be headmaster of the private Pingree School.

XII. THE CAREGIVERS

92. DIRECTOR OF BATTERED WOMEN'S PROGRAM

Salary: $31,500 a year

Hours: 60 a week

Benefits: Health, vacation

Union: No

Experience or Requirements: Volunteer work

Use computer: Yes

Workplace: An office and adjacent meeting room

Risks: Emotional fatigue

Just the other day, a man had gone to the police and accused Prema Vora and her group, called Sakhi, of kidnapping his wife. Vora did not seem particularly worried. Husbands often get angry when Sakhi gives advice to physically and emotionally abused wives. From time to time the husbands get downright threatening with Vora and her co-workers, especially when the wives go to one of the battered women's shelters recommended by Sakhi. Not only does Vora advise the 150 or so women who annually contact her about their legal rights, she also recruits and supervises a cadre of volunteers called advocates, who work one-on-one counseling the battered women. Sakhi—meaning "woman friend" in Hindi—is a nonprofit organization helping women from South Asian countries such as India, Pakistan, Bangladesh, or other countries where South Asians have settled, such as Guyana or Trinidad.

In addition to her other functions, the thirty-year-old Vora raises money from corporate and individual donors. "Next weekend, for example, I'm flying to D.C. to speak to someone about funding." She is also preparing for a "March Against Violence" that her group is sponsoring in Queens, where a majority of South Asian immigrants in the city live.

Vora is the program director. The program coordinator resigned the day before Vora was interviewed, and now Vora finds herself doing the work of two, and also beginning the time-consuming task of finding a replacement for the coordinator. Because her dedication to the job is such that she gives her home phone number to the battered women she helps, the line between home and work is often blurred. "Sometimes when I'm at home and pick up the phone I say, 'Hello, Sakhi.'"

Many others who work with battered women have degrees in social work, but Vora is a professional activist and community organizer. Born in India but raised in the United States, she visited India upon graduation from college and while there decided to devote herself to issues facing South Asian women. Back in New York, she worked first as a volunteer with Sakhi and was pursuing a graduate degree in anthropology, but then she became a full-time employee in August of 1994 and abandoned her academic plans. "I don't look on my job as a job. I feel it's my life's work, in a sense." The life's work is intense, and the tales of the battered women who drop by her Manhattan office are often heart-wrenching. "We're working with one woman right now. In September of '95 she was doused with gasoline and set on fire by her abuser, her husband." His trial is to begin in a week.

Vora says she believes everyone working with battered women goes through periods of great emotional stress, times "when the frustration and the depression become so overwhelming that you lose hope." People in such jobs must be gentle with themselves, she says. "My mom's a psychiatrist, and she says one of the things you have to do is take a vacation every three weeks, just get away for a week." Vora, who lives in Brooklyn and travels by subway to the office, cannot get away every three weeks. But she does take four weeks of vacation a year, and she tries, as well as she can, to keep despair at bay. "Because once you lose hope," she says, "it's all over."

93. EPISCOPAL PRIEST

Salary: About $26,800 a year

Hours: All day, 5 days a week

Benefits: Health, pension, housing, vacation

Union: No

Experience or Requirements: Degree from divinity school

Use computer: Yes

Workplace: Church and community

Risks: Challenges too great for a single soul

On a weekday morning the Rev. Robert Castle might be signing checks or looking over a budget. Afternoons and evenings might find him doing other administrative chores. That bothers Castle, the pastor of St. Mary's Episcopal Church in Harlem, because he did not become a priest more than thirty years ago to push paper. "My strength is more in the street," he says. Weeks away from his seventieth birthday and increasingly reflective, Castle still "fights the good fight," even as he stoically tackles the menial chores. Across the street from the church is the AIDS treatment center that Castle established. The center has a budget of over $7 million and forty beds for area men and women infected with the virus. A food program is also based at the center.

Castle has labored to attract recent immigrants to his church. Sunday masses are conducted in English at 8:00 A.M. and 10:00 A.M., but in Spanish at noon, and in French and Haitian Creole at 2:30 P.M. There are about 500 people in the congregation, and Castle continually pleads with them to confront established power and fight for social and economic justice. An ongoing concern of Castle's has been the disparity in pay between the more privileged priests in the Episcopal Church and those who toil in the vineyards of poverty-stricken areas. Priests are paid by their parishes, which means the priests in wealthier communities earn more money, receive better pensions, and have more benefits than those in poorer ones. "The bishop makes over $100,000 a year, plus all the perks," Castle says. "I've always made the minimum wage of the diocese, $26,800 a year." He says that once, at a diocesan convention, he offered a formal proposal for the bishops "to be an example and reduce their salary," sending the extra money to needy church members in South Africa. "It was put to a vote and defeated," he says.

Castle lives in the nearby Fort George section of Manhattan, but also has a home in Vermont, where he is setting up a summer camp for underprivileged children from New York City. In recent years he has gained a bit of notoriety for minor roles he played in films made by his cousin, director Jonathan Demme. In *Philadelphia* he was the father of the person with AIDS, played by Tom Hanks, and in *Beloved* he played a German store owner who fires Sethe, played by Oprah Winfrey. For his movie work, Castle says he generally earns union scale, which is several hundred dollars a day, but he does not work very many days. If he were to retire now, Castle's pension would be so small he would have to find at least part-time work, he says.

The good fight goes on. One big question nags at him, just as it did when he was younger and taking part in the protest marches that landed him in jail many times. "Why is the church operating on a capitalist system, where the priest gets money according to the size of his church, and priests are encouraged to get a bigger, fancier, richer church?" Castle asks. He didn't tender an answer; there was work to be done.

94. HOME CARE ATTENDANT

Salary: $29,000 a year

Hours: 84 and 72 a week, alternating

Benefits: Health, pension, vacation

Union: Yes

Experience or Requirements: College course in home care, home care certificate

Use computer: No

Workplace: Tiny apartment of client

Risks: Change in assignment, which could reduce salary by two-thirds

At eight o'clock in the morning Alberta Faber arrives at the home of her client, eighty-one-year-old Mattie Johnson, who has advanced Alzheimer's disease, and immediately sets about the day's tasks: making Johnson's breakfast, feeding her, changing her diapers, washing the dishes, cleaning the kitchen, and using a hydraulic lift to move her to a more comfortable position in her chair. Faber repeats the sequence at lunchtime and then again after dinner. Not easy work for a fifty-eight-year-old woman, but Faber has been doing it with Johnson for the past seven years. The feedings are especially tedious because Johnson frequently slaps the food away, and sometimes even slaps Faber. Faber says she persists in coaxing Johnson into taking her meals, sometimes spending more than an hour per feeding, because otherwise "she would be skin and bones." Often "to change her Pampers is a wrestling match, because she doesn't help you." The older woman, unable to talk or move about at this stage in her illness, sits during the day in a regular straight-back chair, with another chair propping up her legs. "She really needs a recliner," Faber says. Johnson's care is paid for by Medicaid and Medicare, under a contract with the nonprofit Social Concern Community Development Agency of Queens, which is Faber's employer.

For half an hour or so in the late morning, Faber will sit and rest. In the afternoon, she likes to watch her hour-long favorite daytime television program, Oprah Winfrey's show. Overall, she finds her work tiring but rewarding. "Music attracts her sometimes," Faber says of Johnson. "You know how people can get rhythm. She shifts. And I talk to her. She sometimes gives a response. Sometimes not. I hug her. Some days she smiles and coos." After serving dinner and bathing Johnson, Faber leaves at 8:00 P.M., turning her client over to the next home attendant, who will spend the evening, night, and early morning with Johnson. As far as Faber is concerned, the night work is easier since Johnson is in bed sleeping. Faber, for the moment, is pleased with the sum total of her income. In addition to her hard-earned salary paid by Social Concern, she receives about $17,000 in annual pension payments from twenty-seven years of working as a communications specialist with a city agency, routing phone calls. Even while working for the city, she did twelve-hour days as a home care attendant. "I slept two-and-a-half hours a night," the single mother says, with a soldier's glimmer of pride. "I was able to pay for my house, send my daughter to college, and I wasn't on welfare." But she also paid a price. Several years ago she had a stroke, which sidelined her for three months. Another time she tore a cartilage in her right knee while lifting Johnson and was out of work for six months.

Faber spends six days a week with Johnson, and works a twelve-hour seventh day with another lady in the early stages of Alzheimer's. She has one free day, every other Sunday. She says that if, God forbid, Mattie Johnson were to die, there is no guarantee she would get another client at seventy-two hours a week. New government regulations severely limit the number of hours of reimbursable care. Faber's $29,000 salary could drop below $10,000 upon Johnson's death. Most home care attendants in the city are black and Latino, largely immigrants, although Faber is a native of South Carolina. She lives in the Springfield Gardens section of Queens and gets around mostly by bus. Of her work, she says, "If you're stressed out, this is no job for you. You have to have a belief in God and like what you're doing and like people."

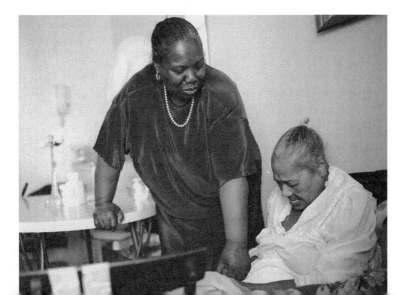

95. CASEWORKER

Salary: $29,000 a year
Hours: 35 to 40 a week
Benefits: Health, pension, vacation
Union: No

Experience or Requirements: Master's degree in education
Use computer: Yes
Workplace: Office and group homes
Risks: Frustration and feelings of guilt

Rose Lanfranchi is responsible for twenty young people, ages thirteen to twenty-one, who are living in group homes on Staten Island. Some are chronic runaways. Others were abandoned by their parents. Most, if not all, are in perpetual need of help, in studying, in staying away from drugs, in surviving from day to day. "We are the first line," Lanfranchi says, describing the role of a caseworker in helping the troubled youngsters lead productive lives. But the forty-three-year-old Lanfranchi agonizes that she cannot do more. The problem is that she has to spend so much time in the office. "I would say 95 percent of our work is paperwork," says Lanfranchi, who drives to work from her home on Staten Island. "It's all about pushing papers."

A visit to her office finds her on the phone with a detective who is inquiring about one of her young people. Chagrined, Lanfranchi admits that she knows little about her. "Most of the time they come in with only the clothes on their back and almost no information," she is saying to the detective. "This girl came into a group home, and I never met her because she ran away before I met her." Upon hanging up the phone, she appears momentarily drained by the conversation. Unfortunately, the details are all too familiar. She says that she takes solace in knowing she does her job well and with integrity. She sometimes goes to the group homes at night, to meet with the youngsters and try to resolve some crisis or merely to stay in touch. And often in the mornings, she visits the schools they attend. She says she does not want any of her "cases" to feel she's in the job just for the money. "There are times I don't get home till eleven-thirty, twelve o'clock at night," she says.

There are a total of fifty-six youngsters in Staten Island living in group homes operated by St. Vincent's Services, the Catholic social services agency that is Lanfranchi's employer, and each home has about nine youngsters. Lanfranchi works out of an office in a ground-floor suite where two other St. Vincent's caseworkers have offices also. Despite her frustration, Lanfranchi says she understands the need to fill out the reports that keep her at her desk and computer most of the day. St. Vincent's receives funding from various sources that require constant streams of documentation. Lanfranchi has also become fluent in the lingo of the social services bureaucracy, using such terms as "PPGs," or "permanency plan goals," which are strategies to ensure that youngsters don't remain in group homes beyond eighteen months. (The caseworkers are supposed to try to get the youngsters either to live independently or with adoptive parents or relatives.)

Lanfranchi makes it clear that the youngsters at the group homes are not on their own. There are a number of professionals who see them on a day-to-day basis, including group "parents" who stay at the homes and monitor activities there, as well as therapists, nurses, and "independent living coordinators," who help the youngsters plan for life on their own. The job consumes Lanfranchi emotionally. "If a child is feeling depressed or wants to see you, I think you should be there," and so she often puts aside her paperwork and dashes off to meet one of her charges. "There has to be a certain level of commitment," she says.

96. SANTERA

Income: $15,600 a year, on average
Hours: 9 a day, 6 days a week
Benefits: None
Union: No

Experience or Requirements: Years of practicing spiritualism in the Dominican Republic
Use computer: No
Workplace: Storefront
Risks: That immigrant believers will lose their faith

Juana de la Cruz says people come to her *botánica* with all manner of problems: a heavyhearted mother with an asthmatic child, a widow in need of consolation, an anguished young man with a wife and a girlfriend. In tending to these ills of body and mind, de la Cruz uses herbs and spiritual practices common among *botánica* owners in the Dominican Republic, where in 1978 she began doing this line of work. She calls herself a *santera*, or priestess. *Botánicas* have flowered throughout New York and other cities over the past two decades, as Latino immigrants have arrived by the tens of thousands. Westerners often view the claims of such spiritualists with great skepticism, but many Latinos, as well as Haitians, are true believers. The icons and statues at de la Cruz's Botánica San Miguel reflect a mix of Catholicism and African beliefs, a syncretism that is common in the Dominican Republic, Haiti, Cuba, and Puerto Rico. "I have helped many people," says de la Cruz, who is fifty years old. "The word spreads and that way I have many clients....Many I charge. Many I don't. It depends on the person. The person may not have anything to pay."

For emotional as well as medical problems, she often prescribes an herb or some other natural substance. She recommends rose honey for blisters and shark oil for asthma but there are many other items in her collection. She often performs a little ceremony, which might be a laying on of hands, or a recitation of a prayer or perhaps the saying of the Rosary. Sometimes the diagnosis, particularly for emotional difficulties, will be done with playing cards. She lays out three piles of cards and has the visitor pick a card from each pile. She puts the selected cards down on the table and makes the sign of the cross before proceeding to "read" the problems in the customer's life. She then offers her advice. "If you have a problem with your wife, you might do a *novena*, nine days of prayer, and you can bring that person closer to you." The key element in any treatment, she says, is faith. She generally charges $20 for a card reading. "There are days when I do twenty cards or more. There are days when I don't do any," she says. "It depends on the problems of the people."

The front of the *botánica* has a glass display case with various religious articles, and throughout the store are crosses, candles, statues of saints, and herbs. A woman comes in and asks for a card with a picture of Mary Magdalene, the New Testament woman absolved of her sins by Jesus Christ. De la Cruz spends a minute flipping through her holdings and comes up empty-handed. "I'm sorry," she says. The woman smiles and departs.

The storefront in which she works is rented for $850 a month by her son, who works a full-time job as a van driver delivering packages. Her assistant is her daughter Wendy, called "Chula," or Pretty One, who attends college and cooks in a kitchen in the rear, several feet from the altar where de la Cruz does her card readings and prayers. The altar is surrounded by lit candles and statues. "I come at 9:00 or 11:00 A.M., and I leave in the afternoon if I don't have many people," she says. "Or I sometimes stay till nine or ten at night." On most days, she goes to and from the *botánica* by private livery cab. The ride takes about ten minutes and costs between five and seven dollars. Speaking of her clients, she says, in Spanish, "They come worried but they leave with a calm heart."

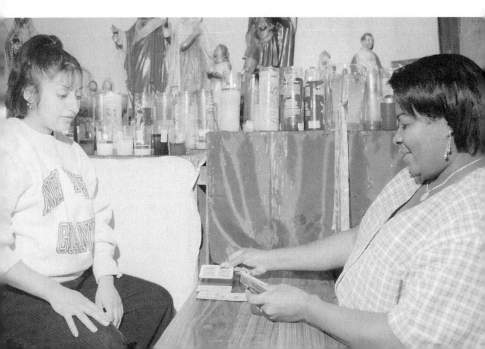

97. HIV CLINIC DIRECTOR

Salary: Above $35,000 a year
Hours: 40 to 50 a week
Benefits: Health, 403B investment plan, vacation
Union: No

Experience or Requirements: Volunteer work and master's degree in public health
Use computer: Yes
Workplace: Large building with clinics and social service programs
Risks: TB exposure

With the widespread use of protease inhibitors to treat AIDS, some people think the AIDS crisis is all but over. But Steve-Albert shows up at work knowing different. True, he says, fewer people are dying from AIDS, but large numbers continue to become infected every day with the HIV virus that causes AIDS. So the crisis is far from over. As director of the HIV, clinic at the Callen-Lorde Community Health Center, which serves New York City's gay and lesbian community, Steve-Albert tries to make life easier for those who have become infected. He oversees staff and volunteers working with 350 HIV patients.

Every weekday, Steve-Albert's clients come to see medical professionals or "peer volunteers," who act as counselors. Steve-Albert says that young gay men in particular have to be informed about safe sex, so that they can avoid being infected with a range of sexually transmitted diseases like syphilis and gonorrhea, or with another strain of HIV, which can complicate their treatment. Sometimes the patients who call or visit are suicidal. Several doctors do exams and prescribe medications.

A significant portion of Steve-Albert's time is spent on administrative chores, filling out reports, and supervising staff. But what he loves most is working directly with the counselors and the clients. He sees his work as a calling more than a job. "I think it has to be someone who is incredibly committed to the fight to cure AIDS and to manage AIDS. I sometimes think it has to be someone who is greatly affected or infected by HIV." Nine years ago, Steve-Albert's partner, Alberto Perez, Jr., who had been a teacher at a public school in Harlem, died of AIDS at the age of 36. Wracked with guilt over his lack of involvement in the AIDS activist movement, Steve-Albert, a former chef, began doing volunteer work at the Community

Health Project. The project changed its name in 1998 to Callen-Lorde, after Michael Callen, an early AIDS activist who died of the virus, and Audre Lorde, a poet who died of breast cancer. The center has a six-story building with 27,000 square feet of rooms and offices, and it offers medical and recreational programs for thousands of gay men and women. Within these walls, Steve Albert has found his new vocation.

In memory of his partner, he began calling himself Steve-Albert, rather than his given name, Steve Stemplewski. In good weather, Steve-Albert, who is forty-four, bicycles from his home in Tribeca. In bad weather, he takes the subway. One of the risks of working at Callen-Lorde is the possibility of picking up tuberculosis. "We have TB tests annually," he says, "and quite frankly I do fear that coming back positive. Because as you know, TB is an airborne infection."

The project receives funding from government and private donors, and it is a decent place to work, the clinic director says. Employees and volunteers are warned to avoid burnout, and Steve-Albert gets four weeks' vacation a year. "No one is standing over me forcing me to work a twelve-hour day, a fourteen-hour day. We could. And if we did they would probably frown upon it. They really encourage us to work a normal eight-hour day. And I think that's out of respect, knowing that the kind of work we do is difficult."

98. EMERGENCY ROOM NURSE

Salary: About $55,000 a year
Hours: 12-hour shifts, 3 days a week
Benefits: Health, pension, vacation
Union: Yes

Experience or Requirements: Degree in nursing
Use computer: Yes
Workplace: Large area with patients, medications, and vials of blood
Risks: Viruses

By his own account, Robert J. Kelly is a cool guy. Handles pressure well. But sometimes the sheer volume of work gets to him. One fall morning finds him taking care of patients in five beds along the west wall of the emergency room at Beth Israel Medical Center. "We turned over those five beds about fifty times, me and Cindy, in a twelve-hour shift," Kelly says. Cindy is the nurse working with him. Amid the noise and bustle, Kelly stands at the bedside of a female patient. The woman's daughter is there, and Kelly begins to ask the daughter questions. Was your mother's speech slurred? Did she seem to be aware of what was going on around her? Was she walking steadily? "You're sort of describing seizures," Kelly says after listening to the replies. Kelly further learns that the woman's son has had similar seizures. He takes her blood pressure. Listens to her heart. Draws blood. Then he spends eleven minutes writing up all that he has learned, concluding that the treatment will probably be the antiseizure medication Dilantin.

Kelly is unusual among nurses, in that he was once a New York City police officer. He spent fifteen years on the job, patrolling the very streets around Beth Israel Hospital where he now works. He took early retirement, became a paramedic, and then a nurse. He said he finds the health field to be "more positive" than police work. But what he really likes about nursing, he says, is the twelve-hour shift, which means a shorter workweek and more days for his personal life. "I can't imagine working five days a week straight." Kelly says the job can be very stressful. "A guy, two weeks ago, I thought he was going to slam me," Kelly recalls, speaking of a patient who

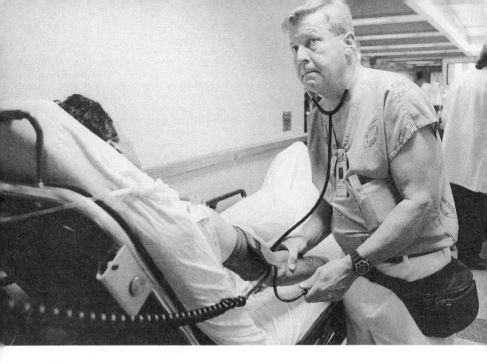

had been diagnosed with AIDS. "He screamed he didn't want me near him anymore....So we had another nurse go in. You know you're sick and not going to get better. Does he have a right to be pissed off? I think so."

Eighty thousand people a year come through the emergency room of Beth Israel. Near the west wall where Kelly works on patients, there are containers marked "biohazard." Little racks of vials, some empty, others filled with blood, are on the table. Activity swirls. Across the room, emergency medical technicians from the fire department come in with a teenage boy who is fighting to get out of the stretcher into which he is strapped. A woman and man who appear to be his parents look distraught and drained. A nurse later discloses that the young man has a history of violent seizures, and this was the latest one.

Taking a coffee-and-cigarette break, Kelly says that he prefers working in the emergency room to working on a ward. He likes staying constantly busy. And he likes the ship-in-the-night quality of the fleeting rapport he establishes with emergency room patients. Speaking of a man he saw earlier in the morning, he says, "He was in the isolation room because he was presumed to be TB. I went in without a mask. I obviously didn't believe he was TB. And it's much more personal."

99. ACUPUNCTURIST

Salary: About $50,000 to $80,000 a year, gross, supplemented with part-time work

Hours: 8:00 A.M. to 5:00 P.M., sometimes evenings

Benefits: Health, self-provided

Union: No

Experience or Requirements: Three years at a school of Chinese acupuncture, master's degree in nutritional sciences

Workplace: Consulting area, room with bed, needles, patients

Risks: Getting stuck with needles

Elaine Retholtz is an acupuncturist and a believer in natural healing. She has her own practice in Manhattan. Before seeing her first patient, Retholtz pulls the charts of all those scheduled for the day. Then she moves on to her favorite part of the job: talking with a patient about her or his problem. "Somebody might come in and say, 'My knee hurts' and I ask them questions." Many are the same questions a physician would ask: How are your bowel movements or menstrual periods? Have you been having headaches? What do you eat and what medications are you on? But she also asks about issues that would concern a psychologist. What is your job like? What stresses are you under? What are your relationships like? She enjoys that part of the job immensely. "I mean I know this person intimately," she says, laughing.

As part of her physical examination, she looks at the patient's tongue, takes the pulse, has the patient lie on a table, and runs her hand sensitively along different ligaments, trying "to feel where it hurts, where it feels empty, where the energy is and where it isn't." She next gets to the essence of her craft: putting needles into sensitive points of the body. Normally, she applies about a dozen needles to various "acupuncture points," those parts through which *qi*, or energy, flows. The idea of the ancient Chinese healing art is to harness the body's energy and channel it, to make the patient better. "I'll turn on some music and leave the room. I leave them for twenty minutes or so.... And then I usually go talk to somebody else. So I use two rooms, and in the middle of talking to that (second) person I'll say, 'Oh, excuse me, I just have to take needles out.'" After removing the needles she consults with the patient, offering dietary and other advice, and scheduling a follow-up visit.

It may take three months before it is clear a treatment is having an effect. But often signs of improvement appear quickly: "Somebody that always has cold hands and cold feet all of a sudden doesn't; somebody who had night sweats, maybe they don't anymore." Retholtz says acupuncture is "absolutely miraculous" in treating sports injuries.

On a busy day, the forty-six-year-old Retholtz will see up to ten patients. The three-year program that she finished at the Tri-State Institute of Chinese Acupuncture, formerly located in Connecticut, now in Manhattan, involved the study of herbs, says Retholtz, who has long had an interest in Eastern religions and meditation. She believes the chances of a careful health provider being stuck by a needle and becoming infected with a virus are low. Generally, she does not wear gloves when applying the needles.

She commutes to her office from her home in Queens, where she lives with her three children, all in college. Retholtz splits the $2,800 rent with seven other women professionals. She has another $9,000 or so in annual expenses but supplements her income working on Wednesdays as an acupuncturist with an AIDS clinic. She does not want to disclose that salary. Of her private practice, she says, "I don't have a receptionist or anything like that. I don't have anyone taking care of the supplies or taking out the garbage. I do everything."

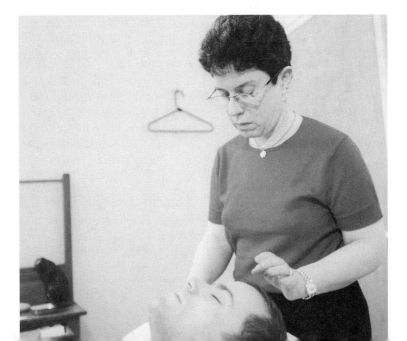

100. EMERGENCY MEDICAL TECHNICIAN TRAINEE

Salary: Volunteer, with potential to earn $24,000 to $45,000 a year

Hours: 40 a week

Benefits: None

Union: No

Experience or Requirements: Classwork and internship with ambulance corps

Use computer: No

Workplace: Office and ambulance

Risks: Infections

Lisa Lashley puts in forty hours a week as a volunteer paramedic trainee at Tri-Community Volunteer Ambulance Corps in Brooklyn's Bedford-Stuyvesant section. At the age of twenty-one, she has done work that would scare the fainthearted. "There's always a call to go to…stabbing victims, gunshot victims…the whole nine yards," she says. "All I've done so far is help with lacerations to the head, and seizures, and people with breathing trouble. I observe. I help with the prehospital report. What time was it? What were the vital signs? I take the blood pressure." In return for her volunteered time, Tri-Community has been paying for her five-month course at the London Agency in downtown Brooklyn, where twice a week she attends classes in emergency medical care. She has been going to the school on Tuesdays and Thursdays from 6:00 P.M. to 9:30 P.M. in the evenings.

"EMTs [emergency medical technicians] usually make good money, from what I've heard, and you can go to work with the fire department, and I suppose that's even more money," she says. EMTs with the New York City Fire Department start out at about $24,000 a year and earn $32,000 after five years on the job. After becoming an EMT, an employee can take 1,200 additional hours of coursework, about a year of part-time study, and become a paramedic. Paramedics, who can administer medication, earn about $10,000 more a year than EMTs.

Most of the trainees at Tri-Community do not fulfill their dreams, an administrator of the volunteer corps acknowledges. Many have troubled home lives and eventually drop out of the program. But Lashley, an immigrant from the Caribbean island of Barbados, says she will make it. Even before starting at Tri-Community, she was getting experience in the medical field, by doing hourly work at a home care agency, feeding and washing the elderly. "I have confidence in myself. I've been working [before] with…blood, feces, whatever," the Brooklyn resident says. "I know how to protect myself, using plastic gloves, washing my hands, making sure I don't have any nicks or cuts."

Anthony Sligh, a vice president of the Community Ambulance Corps, says the corps gets as many as two dozen emergency calls a day. His trainees tend to be young, like Lashley. They often must be drilled in basic people skills, he says. "We train them in CPR [cardiopulmonary resuscitation] and first aid, and we have lectures to instill in them morals, ethics, and respect and to give them what they'll need to go out working in the field once they finish," he says. "So if you'd like to become a paramedic, a doctor, a nurse, a lab technician, just about any job there is in the medical field, this can be a base foundation." It was just this pitch that appealed to Lashley, who was thinking of emigrating to England if she didn't soon put herself on a promising career path. Until fairly recently, the vast majority of trainees at the Ambulance Corps have been men, Sligh says. But more and more women have been coming to the offices to inquire. "I guess they're coming to look at it as a field that's no longer a field for men," he says. "It's a respected type of career."